The OLD BREWERY BAY

ONTARIO
Heritage
BOOK
AWARD

This publication has been assisted by an Ontario Heritage Book Award
from the Ontario Heritage Foundation, an agency of the
Ministry of Tourism, Culture and Recreation

The OLD BREWERY BAY
A LEACOCKIAN TALE

JAMES A. "PETE" McGARVEY

To Val —
Welcome to my Mariposa memories
Best wishes
Pete McGarvey
Mar. 18/06

Dundurn Press
Toronto & Oxford

Editor: Michael Power
Printed and bound in Canada by Best Book Manufacturers

The author and publisher are particularly grateful to the Ontario Heritage Foundation, an agency of the **Ontario Ministry of Culture, Tourism and Recreation,** for a research grant and a grant in aid of publication.

The publisher wishes to acknowledge the generous assistance and ongoing support of the **Canada Council,** the **Book Publishing Industry Development Program** of the **Department of Canadian Heritage,** the **Ontario Arts Council,** and the **Ontario Publishing Centre.**
   Care has been taken to trace the ownership of copyright material used in the text (including the illustrations). The author and publisher welcome any information enabling them to rectify any reference or credit in subsequent editions.

J. Kirk Howard, Publisher

Canadian Cataloguing in Publication Data

McGarvey, Pete
   The Old Brewery Bay : a Leacockian tale

Includes bibliographical references.
ISBN 1-55002-216-4

1. Stephen Leacock Museum – History. 2. Leacock, Stephen,
1869–1944 – Homes and haunts – Ontario – Orillia.
3. Literary landmarks – Ontario – Orillia. I. Title.

PS8523.E15Z83 1994   C818'.5209   C94-932520-1
PR9199.2.L42Z83 1994

Dundurn Press Limited	Dundurn Distribution	Dundurn Press Limited
2181 Queen Street East	73 Lime Walk	1823 Maryland Avenue
Suite 301	Headington, Oxford	P.O. Box 1000
Toronto, Canada	England	Niagara Falls, N.Y.
M4E 1E5	OX3 7AD	U.S.A. 14302-1000

CONTENTS

For Eileen,
at my side today as she was
when this adventure began

FOREWORD

During his lifetime Stephen Leacock was regarded by many of Orillians as an eccentric who had caricatured prominent local citizens in his *Sunshine Sketches of a Little Town*. They ignored his reputation as an academic, a lecturer, an author and a wit with an international reputation. When he died in 1944, it was felt that the Orillia connection would simply fade away.

Quite the opposite has happened. Leacock in some ways is better known now than he was in his lifetime. The story of how this has come about is related in this chronicle by Pete McGarvey. In it, the mythical Mariposa and the real Orillia seem at times interchangeable.

That pleases McGarvey, who is an enthusiast for both Leacock and Orillia. His Leacock crusade dates back to when he was a nineteen-year-old rookie radio reporter in 1947, covering the first Stephen Leacock Medal Awards Dinner for the year's best book of humour by a Canadian author. The annual award was established by a group called the Stephen Leacock Memorial Committee (later known as the Leacock Associates). The medal was designed by Emanuel Hahn and has been bestowed every year with one exception for the past forty-seven years. The seeds of enthusiasm for Stephen Leacock and his Orillia roots were sown at that dinner.

McGarvey was hooked, although there were mishaps at the affair. For instance, the medal hadn't arrived and the first recipient, Harry Symons, author of *Ojibway Melody*, was presented with an empty box. The guests, many of them Leacock contemporaries, such as B.K. Sandwell and Louis Blake Duff, joined in the spirit of the occasion and made it a hilarious happening. McGarvey relates highlights of the various medal awards since and pays tribute to the sheer hard work expended by so many volunteers.

Stephen Leacock had spotted the property known as Old Brewery Bay as a very young man and had never forgotten it. By 1908 he was financially secure so far as income was concerned, and he purchased 19.73 lakefront acres of land surrounding the ruins of an old brewery. The name didn't help his relations with some Orillia critics, but Stephen, with a twinkle in his eye, called it a lure for visitors. Everyone agreed that it was a sylvan delight with a remarkable view. The first building was a crude lean-to at the water's edge, dubbed the "cookhouse." A spacious cottage followed in time, and in 1928 he built the handsome nineteen-room summer home visitors see today. He called the big house, and the gardens, farm and orchard that went with it, "The Old Brewery Bay."

When Pete McGarvey saw the estate for the first time in 1949 it was a heartbreaking sight. In the five years since the humorist's death it had been vandalized, windows broken, roof leaking ... everything in mustiness and decay, including valuable files of Leacock material.

It wasn't a promising scene but it didn't discourage McGarvey. He admits that while desolation marked the site he was affected by the place and the "still apparent, original, beautiful contours."

Recognizing the importance of the property and acquiring it were two different circumstances. The book chronicles the hard work and often disappointing efforts of the volunteers who were as convinced as Pete McGarvey that they had to have the property if any kind of living memorial was to be provided.

Leacock would have loved the plot line of the story, not to mention the improbable cast of characters. In the first place Stephen Leacock Jr., a brilliant eccentric, owned it. He didn't think Orillians had shown his father enough respect, and he ignored the dilapidated condition of the home, asking $50,000 for it.

The Leacock Home Committee, formed in October 1954 with McGarvey as chairman, dealt with one obstacle after another – the town of Orillia's rejection of young Stevie's offer to sell, a later sale to mining magnate Victor Wansbrough that proved to be no sale, and the genuine sale to scandal-sheet publisher Lou Ruby, who saw the property as a housing subdivision. The committee's fortunes turned around when Ruby had a change of heart and offered to sell the home and its priceless literary treasures for $25,000, half the price he paid for the entire property. McGarvey singles him out for praise along with Professor Ralph Curry from Kentucky, who served as curator for a pittance. Newspaper editor C. Harold Hale comes across as a hero. He was a strict temperance advocate who chose to overlook Stephen's advocacy of spirits.

One senses McGarvey's satisfaction in getting the story on record and the fact that it was a personal crusade for him. In a country inclined to the benign neglect of cultural heroes, the lessons of positive involvement of so many people in the Leacock medal awards as well as the rescue and restoration of The Old Brewery Bay should serve as inspiration for other similar efforts.

Harry J. Boyle
Toronto, July 1994

Chronology

1869 30 December: Stephen Butler Leacock born in Swanmore, Hampshire, England.

1876 Leacock family emigrates to a farm in Georgina Township on Lake Simcoe.

1895 Mrs. Agnes Leacock moves to Orillia. Her son, Stephen, soon discovers Old Brewery Bay on Lake Couchiching.

1900 Leacock marries Beatrix Hamilton.

1908 Leacock pays $1600 for 19.73 acres of land fronting on Old Brewery Bay. He is appointed head of the Department of Political Science and Economics at McGill University and helps found the University Club of Montreal.

1915 Stephen Lushington Leacock (young Stevie) born.

1925 Beatrix (Trix) Leacock dies.

1928 Leacock builds his dream house facing Lake Couchiching, 270 feet south of former cottage. He names his estate "The Old Brewery Bay."

1936 Leacock retires from McGill University at the age of 65. He begins to spend more of each year at The Old Brewery Bay.

1944 28 March: Leacock dies of throat cancer in Toronto. 21 June: Stephen Leacock Memorial Committee organized in Orillia at the urging of *Packet* editor C.H. Hale.

1947 13 June: First Leacock Medal for Humour presented to Harry Symons, author of *Ojibway Melody*.

1949   The Old Brewery Bay is leased to Henry Janes, a Leacock family
        friend. Stephen Leacock Jr. cancels lease in October after
        Montreal Standard story suggested that he had neglected his
        father's property.

1953   10 July: Orillia Town Council rejects proposal to send *Sunshine
        Sketches of a Little Town* to London as Coronation gift.

1954   October: The Stephen Leacock Home Committee formed to
        support acquisition and restoration of The Old Brewery Bay.
        Pete McGarvey named chairman. Town council splits on offer to
        purchase entire Leacock estate for $50,000. Stephen Leacock Jr.
        reacts angrily, withdrawing offer. Committee seeks other buyers.

1955   17 August: Mining executive Victor Wansbrough secures option
        on The Old Brewery Bay. He allows option to lapse four months
        later.

1956   16 March: The Old Brewery Bay sold to Toronto publisher
        Louis W. Ruby. He agrees to sell house and adjoining parking
        area to Leacock Home Committee for $25,000 and donate
        home's memorabilia. Offer is open for one year. November:
        McGarvey makes town's purchase of Leacock home a platform
        issue in municipal elections. 10 December: Orillia council passes
        motion to negotiate purchase of Leacock home.

1957   March: Council completes purchase. Louis Ruby presents home's
        contents – over 30,000 items – to town as personal gift. Leacock
        Home Committee dissolved and restoration of home placed in
        hands of Orillia Parks Board. Ralph Curry named as curator.
        June: Orillia Parks Board appeals to National Historic Sites and
        Monuments Board for assistance.

1958   23 January: Northern Affairs Minister Alvin Hamilton pledges a
        $15,000 federal grant when bureaucratic error comes to light.
        Restoration proceeds. June: Town of Orillia by-law establishes
        Stephen Leacock Memorial Home Board with McGarvey as
        chairman. 5 July: The Old Brewery Bay opened with golden key.
        C.H. Hale and Alvin Hamilton share honours.

1959   16 April: Toronto *Telegram*'s "Meet the Authors" Dinner raises
        funds for restoration of sun porch. 4 July: Queen Elizabeth and
        Prince Philip visit Orillia. Town's official gift is *Sunshine Sketches
        of a Little Town*. The Queen reads and enjoys book during stay
        in Yellowknife.

1960   Long-term plans approved for The Old Brewery Bay. Town agrees to settle deficit. Sun porch reopened 11 June on Leacock Medal Dinner weekend.

1977   Ralph Curry retires as curator of Leacock Museum, succeeded by Jay Cody.

1993   31 December: Jay Cody retires as curator of Leacock Museum, succeeded by Daphne Mainprize.

1994   17 June: Swanmore Hall opened as archival and visitor centre. 26 June: National Historic Sites and Monuments Board designates The Old Brewery Bay a National Historic Site in ceremonies at the home.

INTRODUCTION

This book is not a definitive history of either Stephen Leacock or The Old Brewery Bay, or of Leacock's special affinity for Orillia and the Lake Simcoe/Lake Couchiching area. We do not lack for Leacock biographies or published appreciations of his genius. And historians and scholars are waiting in the wings to add to the lore. What I attempt to relate is how the town of Orillia, in the mid-1950s, finally came to terms with its Leacock legacy and its Mariposa alter ego. The town I came to in 1947 as a teenage broadcaster had little use for its Leacockian past. It was not lingering hostility over *Sunshine Sketches*, as non-Orillians assumed. That was ancient and exaggerated history. It was mostly indifference, combined with the resentment of some who recalled that while the country was in dire poverty and still officially dry, and Orillia was under local option, the well-to-do gathered and the booze freely flowed at The Old Brewery Bay. People talked. Rumours spread.

Charles Harold Hale, an upright, God-fearing, temperate Orillian, is the hero of this book. By rights he should have led the forces of righteousness against Leacock and his ways. Instead, he took the true measure of the man years before the rest of the world caught on and never wavered for a moment in his admiration, appreciation and loyalty. In the improbable adventures that led to Orillia's acquisition of the Leacock home, he was my mentor, my partner and my friend. A better one I've never known.

I owe thanks to many people. David Staines encouraged the project from the very beginning, gave his counsel generously and reviewed the manuscript on several occasions. Many people helped in my research, but especially Elizabeth Kimball, William Latimer, Hilary Russell of Parks Canada, Mike Filey of the Toronto *Sun*, Ralph Curry, Jay Cody and Daphne Mainprize. The last three have been successive curators at The Old Brewery Bay over a span of thirty-eight years. Much of the material came from musty boxes in my garage – letters, memos, minutes, newspaper articles, tape recordings and printed programs. David Staines contributed Barbara Nimmo's extensive collection of newspaper clippings, which filled in many gaps in my own clippings file. Fran Richardson at the Orillia Public Library helped me track down early copies of the *Packet* and Daphne Mainprize gave freely of her time and expertise as I sorted through documents and photographs at the Leacock Museum. I'm grateful for the unflagging support of Jeanette Oaten and the Leacock Museum Board, the Stephen Leacock Associates (with particular thanks to Jean Dickson, the tireless chair of the Award Selection Committee) and Doug Little and the Leacock Heritage Festival Board. John Rolland and Peter Rowe added valuable information about everyday life at the Leacock home in the 1930s. I'm indebted to the Ontario Heritage Foundation for generous grants in aid of editing and publishing. Dr. Paul Bator of the Foundation merits special thanks. Michael Power was my editor, and his skilled judgment shows on every page. Thanks go as well to J. Kirk Howard and his professional team at Dundurn Press.

Harry J. Boyle, for many years chairman of the Canadian Radio-television and Telecommunications Commission, composed the Foreword to this book. I met him forty years ago, when I signed on as a correspondent for "Assignment," a ground-breaking news and interview feature he created for the CBC's Dominion network. In 1964 Harry won his first Leacock medal for *Homebrew and Patches*. Ralph Curry and I nominated him immediately afterwards as "The Mayor of Mariposa," and he has filled the office conscientiously for thirty years. His satirical "state of the town" report regales the audience at every medal dinner. Harry won his second Leacock medal for *The Luck of the Irish* in 1976.

My son, Will McGarvey, is responsible for the cover photograph of the Leacock home, as well as the "Leacock's Lakes" sketch and the painting *Summer Comes to The Old Brewery Bay*. As a five year old, he spent a week under the roof of Leacock's lakeside home, convinced that every floor-creak heralded the arrival of a ghost. Now an established Orillia artist, he creates a Mariposa-era painting each year for the Leacock Heritage Festival. His younger brother, Doug, unravelled the mysteries of word processing for me and arranged the manuscript for the publisher as a labour of love.

This book is packed with dates, names and events, a bewildering quantity at times. A chronology has been inserted to help the reader. The difficulty with names starts with the book's title. In the beginning there was Jackson's Brewery on the south shore of Lake Couchiching – a substantial enterprise, according to Sue Mulcahy, whose family goes back to the 1860s in Orillia. The lakeside building was abandoned and eventually fell down. The adjoining inlet, east of Heward's Point, became known, informally, as the "Old

Brewery" Bay. Map makers ignored the name, but Leacock loved it and proudly referred to the "farm" he bought in April 1908 as being located there. In correspondence over the years he often dropped the definite article. When he built the present home in 1928, he retained the article and capitalized it. *The* Old Brewery Bay was the name he settled on for the entire thirty-three-acre estate, house, gardens, orchard and all. He put the name on his stationery – *The* Old Brewery Bay. We copied it in exactly the same type and used it for years after the Leacock Memorial Home, as it was then called, was opened in July 1958. What we called the Leacock Memorial Home is now the Stephen Leacock Museum. Or The Old Brewery Bay, if you prefer.

A word on organizations, another source of bewilderment. The Stephen Leacock Memorial Committee was formed in June 1944 in Orillia, a few weeks after Leacock's death. Under the guidance of *Packet* editor C.H. Hale, it adopted three projects, most notably the annual presentation of the Leacock Medal for Humour. The Memorial Committee became The Stephen Leacock Associates in 1953. The Leacock Home Committee was a separate organization, a citizens group organized in October 1954, to work for the acquisition and restoration of the Leacock home. Again Hale was the spark plug. Although he drew on the resources of the Memorial Committee, this new committee had its own agenda. Its members represented younger blood; I was its chairman. The Leacock Home Committee was dissolved in March 1957, after the town of Orillia acquired the Leacock home and turned its development over to the Orillia Parks Board. In June 1958, the Stephen Leacock Memorial Home Board came into being through a Town of Orillia by-law. Known now as the Stephen Leacock Museum Board, it administers both the home/museum and the adjoining Swanmore Hall and is responsible for the maintenance of a large parcel of municipally owned parkland around the buildings. In addition to the Stephen Leacock Museum Board and the Stephen Leacock Associates, Orillia boasts a Leacock Heritage Festival administered by the Downtown Orillia Management Board, and an International Poetry Festival, featuring Stephen Leacock Awards. The same Orillians often serve on several of these boards though each enterprise is separate and distinct. Can we blame visitors who give up in confusion?

Leacock's fondness for The Old Brewery Bay and Orillia remained with him all his days. In his final summer (1943) he returned to Orillia/Mariposa in a series of "Sunshine Skits," which were in reality thinly disguised pitches for the war effort. Professor Scott Byron of the "Skits" is obviously Leacock, and what he wrote was not fiction:

> The professor comes up to Mariposa pretty often. He's getting now, just that first touch of old age, like September

frost in a garden that mellows a man and makes him cling to the things he's grown used to. The professor, you see, always comes up to Mariposa for his vacations, and he generally manages to have a fortnight at Christmas; he can usually snatch a week for the trout-fishing in May, and likes the break of a fortnight in early June for the herring fishing. Beyond that he has to content himself with odd weekends. He's a busy man. He says so himself. In fact, he's getting touchy about it.[1]

PROLOGUE

STEPHEN LEACOCK, 1869–1944

BY RALPH CURRY

CURATOR EMERITUS, STEPHEN LEACOCK MUSEUM

Born in "exactly the middle year of Queen Victoria's reign" (1889) Stephen Butler Leacock was both a nineteenth- and a twentieth-century author.

Stephen's father, Walter Peter Leacock, tried farming at three different places before he finally gave up and turned to his natural calling – remittance man. In succession, he tried farming in Mariztburgh, South Africa, in Kansas, and in Ontario. Between the first two abortive attempts, he returned to England to study farming by "drinking beer under the tutelage of Hampshire farmers who, of course, could drink more than he could." Here, in Swanmore, Stephen Leacock was born on 30 December 1869.

Stephen Leacock first saw Canada in the spring of 1876, when he came to Canada with the rest of the family to join his father, who had already settled on a hundred-acre farm near Sutton, Ontario. The roomy house was big enough for all eleven children, though cutting wood for the nine stoves was a time-consuming chore. The older children attended "a little red schoolhouse" near the farm until Agnes, Leacock's mother, decided the children were losing their Hampshire accents and installed a tutor in a classroom at the farm.

Young Stephen learned to fit into Upper Canada life. He did his work on the farm, but he swam in, and sailed on, Lake Simcoe. He played cricket at Sibbald's Point; he saw construction of the lovely little Church of Saint George the Martyr finished. He watched the lake steamers handle the commerce of the region, and he saw the railroad come to Sutton and Jackson's Point, ultimately to replace those same steamers. And when he had learned all his tutor had to teach him, he enrolled, with two brothers, in Upper Canada College, his first real connection with the formal education that would occupy him the rest of his life.

At Upper Canada College, young Leacock met a more sophisticated life than he had known before. Here was the life of the city. Here was the world of popular journalism, including the comic magazines which were to play such a role in his career. Here was algebra. Here was a school paper, *The College Times*, for which he could and did write. Stephen quickly outdistanced his brothers, who shortly left Upper Canada College; and he presently outdistanced the rest of the students, being "head boy" in 1887, the year of his graduation.

In the same year, Stephen saw his father for the last time. At the age of seventeen, he was the oldest son still at home. Walter Peter had been in and out since 1878, siring children and leaving them to the care of Agnes. In 1887 Stephen could no longer accept his father's treatment of his mother. He drove his father to the train station in Sutton, put him on a train, and, brandishing the buggy whip, told him, "If you ever come back, I'll kill you!" From that day. Stephen clearly had to take a responsibility for his mother that the other children did not feel.

In the autumn, he entered the University of Toronto, where he had a very successful year. With his superior training from Upper Canada College, Leacock was granted third-year status after one year at university. But the impoverished state of his mother and younger brothers and sisters weighed on him. Deciding that he had to support himself and help support his family, he applied for teacher training and was assigned to Strathroy Collegiate Institute. He taught at Uxbridge and then went to Upper Canada College as a junior master, where he could also enter university again. Teaching at the college and attending classes at the University of Toronto, he took his B.A. in 1891 in modern languages.

For the next eight years, he doggedly taught languages, and he was finally appointed senior housemaster at the age of twenty-five. Unchallenged by the job, he began to write short pieces for the comic magazines of the time and study political economy on his own. Thorstein Veblen's *The Theory of the Leisure Class* (1899) increased his interest. And he met Beatrix Hamilton, whom he wanted to marry. He left Upper Canada College in 1899 to study for his Ph.D. in political economy at the University of Chicago.

By the time Leacock received his degree *magna cum laude* in 1903, he had moved far towards establishing his life pattern. He had married Beatrix in 1900, and he had started teaching at McGill University as a special lecturer in 1901. His career at the University of Chicago had been distinguished. His students at McGill had been impressed enough to report to their principal their admiration. And his marriage to Trix, as he usually called her, had been singularly happy. When McGill offered him a full-time position, the Leacocks made a permanent move to Montreal.

In 1908, after a world tour for the Rhodes Foundation, Leacock was made head of the Department of Political Science and Economics; he helped found the University Club of Montreal, and he bought Old Brewery Bay, thirty-three acres on Lake Couchiching. Developing these enterprises took a large part of Leacock's energy and time the rest of his life.

He published a text in political science and other serious articles intended to enhance his professional reputation during the first part of his career. And while *Elements of Political Science* (1906) sold well, Leacock began to need more money to live the way he desired. He could not ignore that he had earlier started a small reputation as a humour writer, so he collected the fugitive pieces and submitted them. The publisher of his textbook turned the project down. With courage but no little trepidation, Leacock published his first book of humour himself. John Lane immediately picked it up, published an enlarged edition and introduced Leacock to his audience with *Literary Lapses* in 1910.

In quick annual succession, Leacock turned out some of his most lasting works for that voracious audience: *Nonsense Novels* (1911), *Sunshine Sketches of a Little Town* (1912), *Behind the Beyond, and Other Contributions to Human Knowledge* (1913), and *Arcadian Adventures of the Idle Rich* (1914). But in this last year, 1914, as if to remind himself of his scholarly stance, he wrote three volumes of history. The birth of his only son the next year perhaps strengthened a resolve to do "serious" writing. After *Moonbeams from the Larger Lunacy* (1915) Leacock collected some earlier popular essays into *Essays and Literary Studies* (1916). This mixed call to make the public laugh and make them listen continued through Leacock's life, but the lure of humour was stronger; in only two of the years from 1910 until his death did he not produce a humorous volume for his waiting readers.

The birth of Stephen Lushington Leacock, on 19 August 1915, was a long delayed happiness for Stephen and Beatrix and began the most fulfilling part of Leacock's private life. They went to England on a very successful lecture tour. The book sales soared. *The Unsolved Riddle of Social Justice* (1920), perhaps his most significant serious book, was well received. The First World War ended, and the enrolment in his department began to grow. His books during this time were generally respectable in quality, and at least one, *My Discovery of England* (1922), ranks with his best. However, it was increasingly apparent that young Stephen, because of hormonal problems, was not growing as he should, and early in 1925 Beatrix was diagnosed as suffering from advanced breast cancer. She died before the end of the year.

For the next ten years, Leacock gave himself more to McGill and his scholarly profession than to his comedic one, although he turned out his funny book in nearly every year. During this decade he wrote most of his biographies, much of his literary criticism and economics, and a number of internal contributions for McGill University. He worked more closely with the Political Economy Club, and he pushed his students harder – starting a published series for their M.A. theses. With the help of his niece Barbara Nimmo, he re-established his life and routine.

Leacock, however, was shocked by notification of his forced retirement in 1936. He had turned more and more to McGill for the centre of his life, and the abrupt termination might have devastated him. Instead, it made him angry, and evidently the anger stirred the creative juices in him again. A study of humour, a book about a lecture tour through the West, more funny books – now mixed with a quieter, serious intent – and more serious books – now relieved by gentle humour – poured from his prolific pen. This period produced such different books as *My Remarkable Uncle and Other Sketches* (1942), *Montreal, Seaport and City* (1942) and *How to Write* (1943).

With the outbreak of the Second World War, Leacock frequently turned his talents to patriotic causes, supporting the war effort wherever possible. He wrote for the Victory Loan drives; he wrote to encourage the United States to join with Britain and Canada and, when they did, wrote in appreciation; he wrote of the noble cause of the Allies; and he wrote on the prospects for Canada after the war. He put his automobile up on blocks, determined to use no more gasoline until after the war.

Late in 1943, he began having trouble with hoarseness and difficulty in swallowing. The ailment seemed to respond to treatment at first but then grew steadily worse. When it became clear that he was suffering from cancer of the throat, the necessary operation was scheduled. Meanwhile he went on with his work, although slowly. He finished a manuscript he had under way. He sorted through his papers and on 22 February 1944 wrote a memorandum, which he laid on top of a stack of odd papers:

> Sorted
> All Ready
> None Needed for –
> Barbara's Book.

"Barbara's Book" was a reference to his agreement with his niece to gather his unpublished materials into a posthumous volume which she would edit. She would not need to look through this stack. On March 16 the operation was performed, but at the age of seventy-four, his stamina depleted, he had not the strength to recover. Twelve days later Stephen Leacock was dead.

His had been a distinguished career. He had been awarded seven honorary degrees and three medals for literary excellence. He had written sixty-one volumes in more than a half-dozen fields, more than half in humour, of course. He had produced over ninety articles of a serious and scholarly nature. He had advised prime ministers. But mostly, he had made the world laugh. As *The Christian Science Monitor* said at his passing:

> It is all that a man can ask that his fellows should be unable to remember him without a smile, that laughter should be the ultimate expression of their love.

Note: This essay first appeared in *Stephen Leacock and His Works*, published by ECW Press and reprinted here with permission.

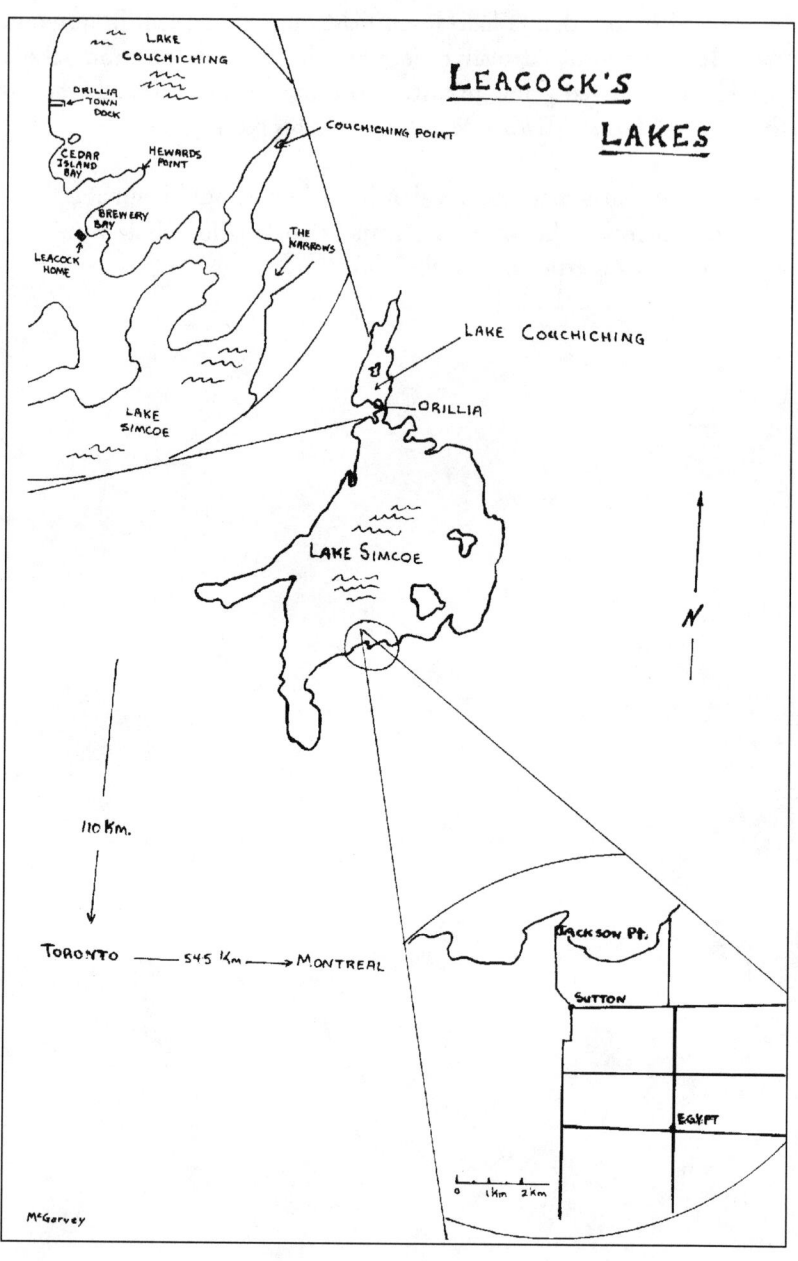

Chapter One

THE OLD BREWERY BAY

One summer's day in the final years of the nineteenth century, Stephen Butler Leacock nosed his sailboat into a secluded inlet at the south end of Lake Couchiching and fell in love. The young language teacher from Upper Canada College was in Orillia visiting his mother, Agnes Leacock, who had moved there in 1895. Sailing was his passion. He had raised his first sail on Lake Simcoe as a teenager. The lake was just six kilometres from the Leacock farm at Egypt, a Georgina Township crossroads five kilometres east of Sutton. By his twenty-first birthday young Stephen had explored most of the east and north shores of a lake he boasted all his life was the most beautiful body of water on earth. With his family's move to Orillia, he explored the Lake Couchiching shoreline with the same thoroughness he had shown Lake Simcoe in earlier years. On the gently sloping southern shore of the inlet were the ruins of an old brewery surrounded by acres of hardwoods – walnuts, oaks and maples. The bay took its name from the brewery. A heavily treed west arm of the bay blocked prevailing westerly winds and the effect was one of utter calm and seclusion. Birds flitted and called through the trees; bass, pickerel, trout and muskellunge darted beneath the dark surface of the water. The bay's east arm, half the length of the west, was low and flat. It, too, was heavily treed and narrowed to a point at its northern end.

On a Sunday stroll with his father, five-year-old Charles Dickens spotted a handsome mansion and declared one day he'd be rich enough to buy it. It was no childish whim. In 1856 he had earned enough through his writing to return to Rochester-on-Medway and buy Gad's Hill Place, his home in the last years of his life. Did Leacock have a similar vision about Old Brewery Bay? Not likely. But he did keep track of the property as his fortunes improved in the first years of the new century. He left Upper Canada College in 1899 to pursue graduate studies in political economy at the University of Chicago. In 1903 he received a minor appointment at McGill University in Montreal, launching what was to be one of the most illustrious teaching careers in Canadian history. And there was more: marriage in 1900 to beautiful Beatrix Hamilton, first cousin of financier Sir Henry Pellatt of Casa Loma fame; a doctor of philosophy degree in 1903; the publication of *Elements of Political Science* in 1906; appointment as an associate professor at McGill the same year; and a tour of the British Empire as a Rhodes lecturer in 1907 at the tender age of thirty-seven! The following year he was installed as chairman of the Department of Economics and Political Science at McGill, a post he would hold for the next twenty-eight years.

He had arrived and he knew it. Royalties from the *Elements of Political Science*, which was soon translated into seventeen languages, and his full professor's salary meant some perks were now within reach. A letter to his mother from Marseilles in May 1907 talks of the need to find some property in the Orillia area to call his own. He asks his brother Charlie to check out "the little point" on Lake Couchiching as a possibility, "if it's not too wet." In an article written in the 1950s, his sister Margaret (Daisy) Burrowes recalls a lovely Easter Sunday in 1908

> ... when Stephen and I met in Orillia and walked out "The Old Northern" track and through the fields where the ruins of the old stone brewery stood, and we picked out the spot where later he built his house. A year before, in 1907, Stephen and his wife, Beatrix had taken a trip around the world, Stephen lecturing for the Cecil Rhodes Scholarship fund, and in the many letters he wrote (mainly to his mother to be shared with the family) while on this tour, he mentioned how he longed to be home again and his desire to buy land near Orillia. In one letter written in September 1907 from Australia, he says, "I am awfully anxious to buy a small place on Lake Couchiching next Spring. I shall try to have enough money for the land and will live on it in tents and shacks for next summer and build on a large scale the year after. I want to have at least ten acres, a sort of small farm, room for a very large garden (Stephen was an enthusiastic gardener), an orchard, a wooded lot and a field of root crop, hen feed and so on. I shall keep hens, a cow – as to a horse – I don't know. It needs so much land to feed off. I must get Charlie to go into it with me."[Charlie was an unmarried

brother, two years younger than Stephen.] "I'll have the place big enough for him to have a cottage of his own (he might not like merely a share in the house) and when I am ready, I will retire to it. When I build my house I shall make it very plain and at the same time very large. I mean to plant a good avenue of trees leading up to it. In a few years with hard work it will begin to look fine. After it has been up two or three years, I shall brick it with white brick and put in lattice windows in place of the original ones and tile instead of shingles on the roof. Then by adding a sundial, a yew hedge, as rook and three wall-flowers, it will become a charming English place. I'm tired of cities and people. It's a case of Goodbye, proud world, I'm going home."[1]

On 15 April 1908, the Montreal professor paid $1600 for 19.73 acres of broken Lot 10, Concession Six of the Township of South Orillia, fronting on Lake Couchiching, "within the town of Orillia." The terminology is confusing but proper. Many written articles on Leacock's summer place later placed it "near Orillia" when in fact it was within town limits from the beginning. The property was part of a fifty-two-acre crown lot acquired in 1856 by lumberman John Thompson. In succeeding decades the lakefront land was subdivided, sold and resold, passing from the hands of one wealthy Orillia family to another. Leacock bought his acreage from the trustees of the estate of Orillia barrister Frank Evans. They took back an $800 four-year mortgage.[2] Later purchases would enlarge the estate to thirty-three acres. In *Stephen Leacock, Humorist and Humanist* Ralph Curry observes that for the rest of his life the three things that he cared for the most were his Orillia "farm" on Old Brewery Bay, the University Club in Montreal and his department at McGill, all of them having their genesis in that fateful year – 1908![3] For Leacock, Old Brewery Bay represented many things: a place for family, a rural retreat from the rigours of university life and public speaking, an estate that could grow as his fortunes improved, and a return to the beloved land and waterscape of his boyhood. Even the name was special to him. Barbara Nimmo, his niece and long-time secretary, writes in her preface to *Last Leaves:*

> He used to say he could judge his visitors by that name. "If they like the name Old Brewery Bay, they're all right. They can have anything on the place. I have known that name, the Old Brewery Bay to make people feel thirsty by correspondence as far away as Nevada.[4]

Winter, spring and fall were spent in a comfortable home on Côte-des-Neiges Road in Montreal. Summertime belonged to Orillia. During Leacock's first summer, the property had but a shanty down by the shore, slapped together by Stephen and Charlie. Later, more brush was cleared and a proper cottage constructed.

In her chronicle, Daisy Burrowes told how two of the Leacock brothers broke ground and started what was to become a never-ending construction program:

> There was great activity the first summer (1908) when Stephen and Charlie built a one-roomed cottage. "Cook House" they called it and we used tents for sleeping. The following year they built a large, partly closed-in verandah across the front with two bedrooms leading off at each end. In the verandah sitting room Stephen put a Franklin stove. Maybe you don't know this type of stove. It has an open-grate front and stands upright with its back to the wall. One fall when I was staying at Stephen's he showed me with pride how he had "built a fireplace and chimney" by enclosing the stove in asbestos. The pipe coming up through the chimney he had painted red, blocked off in black to look like bricks. "It's a very Santa Claus fireplace," he remarked. "Wait till you see it going." We admired it. Then suddenly a flame shot from the chimney. Then another and another. Fortunately, with the lake only a few feet away, a quickly formed bucket brigade soon had the fire under control. Stephen's only comment was "Too bad. Still it worked." And it certainly did! As time went on bigger and better rooms were added, with the first little "Cook House" still the centre of the house. The sitting-room had guest rooms flung out like arms around it. It was hard to realize that the attractive children's dining room had started out so humbly.
>
> "A big house with room for you all," Stephen said to me the day I signed as witness to the deed for the land. It is a happy thing to remember that through his own work he was able to obtain his ambition and, in later years, though we all had homes of our own, we were still sure of a warm welcome at "Old Brewery Bay."
>
> After the death of Stephen's wife Beatrix, in 1925 the large rambling cottage they had planned and built together was torn down and the present house was built. Only then

did the little "Cook House" of 1908 give up the ghost. As I think about it and write, even the new house no longer seems empty and deserted, for I feel that Stephen's spirit must linger near the house he built and his 'Mariposa,' the place he loved so dearly and pictured so clearly in his "Sunshine Sketches of a Little Town."

Daisy Burrowes's daughter, writer Elizabeth Kimball, affectionately recalls the Leacock cottage in *My Uncle, Stephen Leacock*:

> It was long and low, with Aunt Trix's and Uncle Stephen's bedroom at the front, opening, as I recall on the verandah. Leading off this bedroom, or across a narrow hall from it was Stevie's nursery; it, too, opened on the verandah, and one could see the lake from there. Looking back I realize that quite likely one reason I preferred the first house was its proximity to the water ... I do remember a long gallery at the back of the house and I think the children's dining room was at the kitchen end of this. At any rate we ate at the kitchen end of it. I loved that gallery. It had a floor of red tile ... The roof had tiles of the same shade of red. This was my first experience with this delicious shade of red ... And my only recollection of the drawing room was that it had a lot of wicker furniture in it ... The only other room I remember was Granny's bedroom, which was, I think, at the same end of the house as Aunt Trix's and Uncle Stephen's, but in another wing. It led directly outside, so that Granny could get at her beloved outdoors and "garden" without having to go through the house.[5]

The proportions of the cottage were aesthetically satisfying, according to Kimball. Primroses and wallflowers grew in the garden and a sundial was positioned about thirty feet south of the house. On its cement base her uncle had traced the words "Brevas Horas – Longos Annos" (Brief hours, long years).

On 15 May 1908, scarcely four weeks after his property was bought, Leacock introduced himself to a meeting of the Orillia Canadian Club as a "plain farmer, [come] to speak to his fellow citizens."[6] Several snapshots, dated 1912, show tents on the property. Some hand-writing on the back of one of them informs us that it's the year of the diphtheria epidemic. The professor allowed townspeople to camp on his point, to escape the spreading illness, and the little peninsula became known as "Leacock's Camp."

The year 1912 brought more than diphtheria to Orillia. *Sunshine Sketches of a Little Town* appeared that year, the book that was to immortalize Leacock's adopted town as Mariposa and establish him as Canada's foremost humorist. Leacock stated, with tongue in cheek, that his *Sketches* were about no real place or people, but Orillians knew better. The landmarks and characters were obvious. It was a delicious spoof, as well as a masterpiece of insight and style. In "Netley's Store" Orillians recognized Hatley's General Grocers. The *Newspacket* was a combination of the *News* and the *Packet*. There was a "Smith" of enormous girth who ran a local hotel. Barber Jeff Thorpe was barber Jeff Shortt.

For several generations, it has been taken as gospel that Orillians en masse were outraged by this cruel caricaturing of their town and its leading personalities. Leacock's own mother reprimanded him for turning Canon Richard Greene of St. James Anglican Church into the hapless Dean Drone. But Greene, apparently, did not mind. Shortly after the book appeared, he was seated at a Toronto banquet behind the name card "Dean Drone" and laughed along with his fellow diners. Charles Harold (C.H.) Hale, the editor of the Orillia *Packet* for more than a half-century, told me that resentment was limited to only a few people. The truth is that Orillians relished the *Sketches* as much as Canadians elsewhere did. An exception was barber Jeff Shortt. He told a friend, "I used to talk to the fellow while I was shaving him, but I never thought he was going to put it all in a book."[7] "The Sinking of the Mariposa Belle" is described by Hale as an "exaggerated version of an experience in which Leacock himself was among passengers who spent a night storm-stayed in Lake Simcoe"[8] And "The Great Election in Missinabi County" was inspired by an election campaign (in 1911) in which Leacock himself had "stumped the riding."[9]

Hospitality at the Leacock cottage was always hearty, if sometimes haphazard. In Orillia, as in Montreal, the Leacocks loved to entertain. As well as assorted Leacocks, Hamiltons and Pellatts there were often visiting academics, writers and politicians. Among Orillians made welcome at the Leacock cottage were Charlie Janes, a "railway man," George Rapley, the bank manager, and John Drinkwater, a jovial farmer from North Orillia Township, who owned a trout-stream where Leacock fished when time allowed. Guests would often find themselves on their own, if Leacock decided fishing was more interesting than dinner or if Beatrix forgot to check her watch. The birth of Stephen Lushington Leacock in 1915 brought great happiness to his parents. His family called him "Little" Stevie. In later years, he would be known universally as "Young" Stevie. Happiness came to the Leacocks also in glowing reports from Stephen's publishers, not to mention the cheques they enclosed. From 1913 onwards, Leacock published annually a new collection of humour to regale an audience which encompassed virtually every corner of the world. He was Canada's – and the world's – most popular and most successful humorist.

When the First World War ended in 1918, the expansion of Old Brewery Bay resumed. Leacock was a restless builder. He loved to sketch out new "projects" over the long winter in Montreal, then complete them the following summer at the lake. An ice house was an early example. A two-storied boathouse was erected in 1919 on the west shore of the bay. Hen houses, greenhouses and assorted outbuildings for his expanding farm, garden and orchard operations – these would appear one season, only to be altered, moved, or torn down the next. In 1921, he called on the prestigious Toronto architectural firm of Chapman, Oxley and Bishop to design a country home for him based on the rough sketches he and his Montreal friend and Orillia neighbour, Mrs. H.T. "Fitz" Shaw, had drawn. He had estimated a cost of $8,000 if generous use were made of materials from the cottage. The quote was closer to $25,000! Leacock was aghast. The recession then under way gave him an excuse to back off. The Chapman "chateau," designed to be attached to the existing cottage and built on a north-south axis, would have faced Barnfield Bay, the inlet east of the Old Brewery Bay. The plan for a grander home was shelved though not forgotten.

In 1925 Beatrix Leacock died of breast cancer, leaving a grieving husband and a ten-year-old son. Young Stevie's health problems – arrested physical development – only added to his father's woes. Stephen's therapy for grief was work. He wrote tirelessly, continuing both his academic and humorous publications, meanwhile adding his voice and influence, not to mention his finances, to appeals for funds to support cancer research. 1927, he and twelve-year-old Stevie visited Britain then took an extended holiday at Biarritz in the hope that the Mediterranean warmth and sea air would benefit the boy.

Back in Montreal that autumn Leacock returned to his plans for a new home on his Lake Couchiching property. By phone, he handed the assignment to Kenneth Noxon of the Toronto architectural firm Wright and Noxon. Although Leacock at first envisioned elaborate additions to the existing cottage, he later accepted Noxon's better idea – a brand new structure, on a rise 270 feet south of the old cottage. Back and forth went sketches and scale drawings.

For Noxon, Leacock's new home was a dream assignment. By 1928 his firm had completed a number of projects in the Lake Simcoe area, including "Invermara," the Ambrose Small summer home two kilometres east of Old Brewery Bay. And others lay in the future – the Hotel Champlain in Orillia and a summer home and boathouse near Beaverton for Foster Hewitt, the dean of Canadian hockey broadcasters. Noxon was an unabashed Leacock fan. In a letter to Ralph Curry in June 1959, the architect wrote, "You can imagine the astonishment and pleasure I felt when completely out of the blue he phoned me from Montreal asking if I would undertake the work on the house. I could not imagine then and cannot think now of any other individual that I would have preferred to work with."[10]

Noxon's design was inspired. He knew what he had to create – a structure to satisfy a demanding client, and at the same time a home that would convey to future generations a sense of the character of this Canadian genius. It was a tall order.

The home would be 104 feet in length, extending back fifty-six feet in the west and east wings. According to Noxon's 1927 blueprint, four sets of French doors would open onto the first floor from a verandah, twenty-nine feet long and ten feet deep. Eight tapered white wooden columns, joined by wide, lattice-filled arches, would support the verandah's roof. One set of French doors was to lead to the professor's study, identified as a bedroom at that point. To the right of these doors, at the exact centre of the verandah, the home's main door would open onto a short passageway to the sun porch. Stairs leading to the second floor would be located at the south end of the passage, with an additional door to the study at the foot of the stairs. Directly inside the main door on the right the visitor would enter the dining room, which measured sixteen by fifteen feet. It would be the home's crossroads. Five doors in all would lead to it – from the hallway, the sun porch, the kitchen, the verandah and the living room. The living room, twenty-six feet long and sixteen feet wide, was to be the heart of the home, the site of all future socializing. It would narrow into an alcove at the west end. The home's largest fireplace would be located on the living room's south wall. The west wing would be completed by a large kitchen and larder, with entrances from it to both the dining room and sun porch. A door off the kitchen would lead to the servants quarters – a narrow passageway, two tiny bedrooms and a bathroom. The basement stairs would be off the kitchen, directly north of the dining room entrance. Downstairs, a room for English billiards would be situated under the west end of the living room. A wine cellar was to be located opposite the billiard room. The sun porch was to be of the same dimensions as the verandah, thirty nine feet long by ten feet deep. It was to be accessible from the kitchen and dining room on the east side, the main hallway in the centre, the professor's study just east of the hallway, and his private quarters at the further end of the north wall. The door here would be solid wood – all others would be glass – to assure privacy. It would open onto a windowless passageway, leading to a southern bedroom measuring twelve by sixteen feet, and a northern one, sixteen by seventeen-and-a-half feet. To complete the home's main floor symmetry, the larger bedroom would also narrow to an alcove. Two bathrooms and two closets would complete the east wing.

The upstairs was to be completely symmetrical. A narrow hall at the top of the reversing stairway would open onto four bedrooms. The nearest two, east and west of the stairs, would each measure eleven feet, six inches by thirteen feet. Beyond them, at either end of the floor, would be chambers measuring eighteen feet, six inches by fourteen feet. Each bedroom would have its own fireplace and each would open onto a balcony. The largest balcony would be the reinforced roof of the verandah, with a lattice railing at its northern edge. The smaller balconies at either end of the home would feature similar railings. Two spacious bathrooms (eight feet, four inches by nine feet) would be located on either end of the upstairs hallway. The roof would be steep-pitched with dormer windows on four sides. The ridge, eight feet wide and flat, would run sixty-one feet. Seen from above, the home would look like a squat "H."

Leacock liked the blueprint. Orillia contractors E. Webb and Son set to work in May 1928 with a twenty-man crew and the promise of a $1000 bonus if a 1 July deadline was met. In 1982, one of the Orillia workers, Oscar Olimer, remembered "Teddy" Webb recruiting carpenters from as far away as Cookstown. General workers got forty-five cents an hour.[11] Due to Leacock's frugality the house contained much of the original cottage. Six thousand feet of V-Joint sheathing were salvaged and recycled, along with 2000 feet of two-by-four studs, and 2200 feet of floor and roof boards. What remained of the lakeside cottage was retained for future building projects, principally a shelter for the private trout pond in Oro Township Leacock was then leasing.

The professor was proud of his new summer home and more than pleased with the cost – a surprisingly modest $17,463.80! In a letter dated 1 September 1928 he expressed his delight to Noxon:

> I feel that I shall always be in your debt for your brilliant original plan of remodelling or rather rebuilding my house, instead of merely moving and enlarging it. You have made a thing of great beauty and for me a source of pleasure and satisfaction for the rest of my life.

A feature article in the May 1930 *Canadian Homes and Gardens* looks approvingly at the finished structure: "The interior finish is unusual in that there are no plaster walls. Pine sheathing, lightly stained and oiled, has been chosen for all the wall surfaces and the result is similar to the more expensive panelling." The panelling was Norwegian pine, known for its glowing warmth.

Stephen Leacock's fussiness over design and construction didn't extend to furnishings. In *Remembering Leacock*, Dode (Tudhope) Spencer relates:

> We felt we could let ourselves go at the Leacock home, more than we could at our own homes. One thing, it was very summer-cottagey. It was sparsely furnished. Stephen didn't really care about possessions and material things. It was of no interest if he broke glasses. He went out and bought some more. And he didn't have the best crystal or anything; that didn't worry him. Or maybe he might have, but even if he did, and it was broken – so what.[12]

Plain and functional was the rule for furniture. Wicker chairs and settees were everywhere. The slapped-together worktable on the sun porch and the homemade shelving in bedrooms and library confirm Spencer's observations on Leacock's disdain for fancy things.

Elizabeth Kimball remembers a house of Spartan character:

> ... housing on its second floor a collection of iron hospital beds and white enamel basins which were oddly stained with brown. (I say oddly, because how can a basin become rust-stained from whose taps water never flows?) Another interesting feature was the dense army of mosquitos, unequalled in size and ferocity by any other animal save perhaps the tigers of Bengal.[13]

The new home and the surrounding acreage soon had a name – "The Old Brewery Bay," in the manner of an English estate. And Noxon drew a further assignment from his satisfied client. Two years after the main house was completed, he designed a "charming little lodge" for the use of Leacock's housekeepers. Its two main features were a stucco exterior and extensive interior panelling. Leacock paid particular attention to the fireplaces in the lodge. He wrote an Orillia builder in 1930 that "the concrete bases of the fireplaces are to be made ready by me ... the living room fireplace ... is to have one flue in the chimney and a hole in the bricks ... for a stove-pipe. No damper. The height of the chimney must clear the eavestroughing of the cottage ... and the roof ridge roughly 18 feet."[14]

Handsome his new home was, but Leacock was not about to forget that it was also the centre of a farm. A large greenhouse rose at the southeast corner of the house, for tomatoes and lots of flowers. This was the domain of Bill Jones, a retired but still dapper British army sergeant who filled many roles around the place. He was one of the people the humorist had in mind when he wrote:

> Do I do all the gardening myself? Oh yes! There isn't any fun in it if you don't do it yourself. Did I dig it? No, I didn't dig it. That's pretty darn heavy work. Every spring I get a man to dig it and then I get a boy for the weeding and I get a woman in to do the picking. But beyond that, I do the whole thing myself, especially the planning.[15]

A large barn and hen-house went up beside the greenhouse. On the wall of the barn Leacock posted the daily work routines for Jones and whoever else was hired on a seasonal basis. David Rowe and his son Lawrence of Orillia were often on the payroll. Jack Kelly was the overseer. The Belfast-born husband of the Leacocks' housekeeper, Tina Pelletier, Jack was equal to every assignment. He was gardener, repairman, handyman and chauffeur (Leacock never learned to drive). He liked his boss and his boss liked him. Kelly's death in a car crash near Orillia, in September 1939, left a void at The Old Brewery Bay. The Kellys lived in the 1930 lodge; nearby was a second, smaller greenhouse. Stretching west and south of the lodge were the trees that constituted the Leacock orchard. The farm produced a broad range of vegetables and also some hay, the latter for the resident livestock. Chickens, pigs, cows and an occasional horse were sheltered at The Old Brewery Bay in the decade after 1928. A trained economist, Leacock kept meticulous records of his farm and garden operations, though he omitted some costs. At tomato-picking time, for instance, he was known to get the latest price by phone from Hatley's store, then call for a taxi to transport two or three baskets to the grocery on Mississaga Street. The profit from the sale never equalled the taxi fare.

Nephews and nieces were frequent guests at The Old Brewery Bay. One niece, Barbara Ulrichsen (later Nimmo), served as chatelaine of the estate as well as a secretary and companion to her uncle.[16] She had vivid memories of agricultural experiments at the lakeside farm:

> One summer it was Montreal melons, which reached a size of twenty pounds but needed as much care as a new-born baby; another year, turkeys. I remember our dining one Thanksgiving on the sole survivor of a brood of one hun-

dred which, at fifty cents to start plus the feed (until one by one they died) represented a hundred dollars. But Uncle Stephen could always laugh it off, very literally, as he'd often write an amusing story and make many hundreds more. He spoke of his place in a letter: "I have a large country house – a sort of farm which I carry on as a hobby … Ten years ago the deficit on my farm was about a hundred dollars; but by well-designed capital expenditure, by drainage and by greater attention to details, I have got it into the thousands."[17]

In the late spring, the Leacocks, Senior and Junior, Barbara Ulrichsen and the household staff would depart Montreal by motorcade for Orillia. Summer would stretch to well past Labour Day. There were always new ventures in gardening and egg production or construction of a new building. Just as important were the social occasions, the garden parties and picnics, the croquet and cricket and tennis matches, the home-made plays with Stevie and his cousins in starring roles, and the non-stop entertainment of Leacock friends from many spheres. Fishing topped the list of recreational options at The Old Brewery Bay. A call to Jake Gaudaur at the nearby Narrows reserved a guide and a launch. Picnic lunches were packed, along with a jar or two of distilled spirits, and the company was rounded up. "Bass Fishing on Lake Simcoe," a 1930s essay, tells of one such expedition:

> " Will it rain, Jake ?"
> "I don't think so, professor; not with that sky."
> We've gone through this little opening dialogue, I suppose a hundred times. That's the beauty of bass fishing; always doing the same things in the same way, with the same old jokes and same conversation.
> "I was thinking we might go out and try the big rock at McCrae's Point first, professor."
> Seeing that we've never done anything else in twenty years, it seems a likely thing to do.

Old Brewery Bay waters were productive, especially if you knew where and when to cast your line. The professor often bet his guests that he would be the first to net a fish in the bay. His bet rested on some inside information. Leacock knew the location of the springs of an old mattress on the lake bottom. He and handyman Bill Jones placed it there, and attached bait to it. Several times a year the springs were dragged up and the bait replaced.

Leacock always dropped his line on days the mattress was not baited, knowing that hungry bass were circling below.[18] In the 1930s Christmas was a joyous season at The Old Brewery Bay. If weather and schedules allowed, the holiday would stretch to two weeks. Wood fires drove out some of the cold, and so did a drop of whisky. The entertainment was home grown, often a pantomime written by the humorist and played out by the young people present. Leacock kinfolk and guests gathered near the tree, in an alcove at the west end of the long front parlour. Around the crackling fire, the carols were sung, toasts drunk, yarns swapped. René du Roure, Leacock's McGill colleague, dearest friend and billiards companion, was a frequent guest at The Old Brewery Bay. Indeed he was there so often that the larger bedroom in the east wing was considered his personal domain.

When Daisy Burrowes witnessed the deed of purchase in April 1908 her brother Stephen spoke of "a big house with room for you all." Twenty years later, the promise was fulfilled. Elizabeth Kimball writes:

> He only meant the family then, his mother and brothers and sisters. But Old Brewery Bay, although its rooms were only nineteen in number, seemed capable of containing any number of guests … the husbands and wives of his brothers and sisters, the nieces and nephews, hosts and armies of friends. It seemed indeed big enough to contain the whole world. His great, hospitable spirit made it so.[19]

After his mandatory retirement at McGill in 1936, Leacock spent much of his time at Orillia, retreating to Montreal only when November's raw winds invaded his lakefront home. The pattern of his days remained unchanged. Yousuf Karsh told me in February 1992 of a visit to Leacock's Orillia home in August 1941 that stretched from the originally scheduled afternoon to three days. He related how the famous humorist went to bed at mid-evening and appeared at breakfast the next morning with his day's quota of writing completed. On this occasion it was read to the house guests by young Stevie. Karsh recalled the aging humorist as the perfect host, attentive and gracious, a brilliant conversationalist, and one of the most co-operative subjects he had ever encountered. The results of the expedition, Karsh's first venture into extended photography, are among the photographer's finest work. His study of the humorist at his desk in the sun porch is universally accepted as the definitive Leacock portrait. Leacock thought so, too, writing Karsh later and awarding him the "Leacock Gold Medal"![20]

When Stephen Leacock died of throat cancer on 28 March 1944, many felt that The Old Brewery Bay had also perished. The soul and presence of a giant were gone. Young Stevie continued to spend part of each year on the property, living in the 1930 lodge. Neglect also took up residence. As the years passed, the once carefully tended lawns and gardens were overwhelmed with weeds and underbrush, broken doors admitted rain and snow, and the sun porch roof collapsed. Vandals smashed windows, hoboes bedded down overnight and thieves made off with clothing, pots and pans, fortunately leaving behind the far more precious relics of a memorable life. The Old Brewery Bay was rapidly turning into a derelict.

Chapter Two

C.H. HALE, THE CATALYST

C.H. Hale rescued The Old Brewery Bay – with a little help from his friends. A native Orillian, he was the town's grand old man, its principal historian and its unabashed cheerleader. He was a visionary, a born organizer, a shrewd political strategist. His fragile frame, austere manner and gentle speech concealed the temperament of a zealot and a constitution of pure iron. After service to God and country, his overriding mission in life was to transform his beloved Orillia into Canada's model community – Christian, sober, industrious and loyal to the imperial community and the Conservative cause.

George Hughes Hale, Harold's father, a self-educated editor and printer of Anglo-Irish descent from Omemee, a village near Peterborough, arrived in Orillia the same day Canada was born, 1 July 1867. Three years later, he and his brother William launched the *Packet* as a Conservative voice in a village served till then only by a Liberal newspaper. Nine columns wide, the *Packet* featured poetry, advertisements and uplifting English novels on page one and devoted pages two to four to the most microscopic examination of local life any journal has ever published in Ontario. The Hale brothers spent the next half-century fighting the demon rum, municipal corruption and the Liberals in a town just then emerging from the rough-and-tumble lumbering era. Week by week, from 1870 to the turn of the century, they exposed Orillia's liquor law infractions and civic sins with thundering righteousness. Although locals relished the editorial fulminations, they had little impact on people's private behaviour. There is no evidence whatsoever of a decline in Orillia's alcoholic intake during the heyday of the Hale brothers.

If the paper had been merely a temperance scold, it would have folded within a year or two, as many journals did in those days. Its salvation lay in its exhaustive community coverage and a rare literate quality. News columns read like pages from such British essayists as Addison, Lamb and Macauley. Its grammar was impeccable; typos almost non-existent. Moreover, it scanned a much broader horizon than little Orillia. The *Packet* was Tory and imperialist to the core. *Packet* commentaries on national and imperial questions were followed with interest by Macdonald government ministers in Ottawa and, according to the rumour mill, by the occupant of 10 Downing Street in far-off London! Reports of such recognition delighted the brothers, who were anglophiles to their fingertips. For years George Hughes Hale also penned a column of temperance tidings for an English magazine where he gave his address as "Near Rugby, Canada." The name Orillia, Ontario, would mean nothing to an English readership. But Rugby, with its old school connotation and its association with Dr. Thomas Arnold and his son Matthew, suggested an upper-class and education-conscious neighbourhood. The joke, of course, was on the English magazine. Canada's Rugby was a dusty little hamlet, a few miles west of the equally dusty Orillia.

When C.H. Hale became the *de facto* editor of the *Packet* in 1900 he quietly changed the paper's mission. Temperance, Empire, and God were still on the first page but he also published stories selling the merits of inexpensive, locally produced hydro power as the key to Orillia's industrial prosperity.[1] The Orillia Power Scheme of 1898 was Hale's first major community campaign and it succeeded brilliantly. Five years before the formation of Ontario Hydro, Orillia was generating all the current needed by a brace of new foundry industries, with enough left over to light up the main street. Orillia's "Golden Age" was at hand, and C.H. Hale was its principal architect. Industrialists, profiting from cheap electricity, became Orillia's chief benefactors and major contributors to Hale's many causes: the YMCA, the Carnegie Library, the Board of Trade, the Canadian Club, the Soldiers Memorial Hospital and the magnificent Champlain Monument, which was unveiled in Couchiching Beach Park on 1 July 1926.

It was Hale who proposed in 1913 a monument to mark the 300th anniversary of Samuel de Champlain's arrival in Huronia. He organized the financial drive, coaxed a $12,500 grant out of the federal government towards the $20,000 cost, helped choose the winning design and directed the unveiling. On hand that happy day were leading federal and provincial politicians speaking both official languages (the monument was intended to symbolize the unity of Canada's founding races), representatives of First Nations bands in full regalia, and a cast of locals costumed as the intrepid French explorer and his retinue. Stephen Leacock was also there. He spoke about the life of Orillia's first European visitor and of Canada's unique cultural heritage. For Orillia it was a day of button-bursting pride. For Charles Harold Hale it was just one more campaign. His story on the unveiling carries no hint of his seminal role in the project. Instead he gave credit to dozens of others. Hale's modesty was as genuine as it was rare. Like every other Hale project, the Champlain Monument has passed the test of time. Designed by Vernon March of Farnsborough, England, at the age of twenty-one, it is undoubtedly a masterpiece. March later created the National War Memorial in Ottawa.

Hale first met Stephen Leacock before the turn of the century but not in Orillia. The two were keen cricketers playing for rival teams in a Lake Simcoe league. Their first encounter was probably at a match in Beaverton in the mid-1890s. In a 1957 Canadian Broadcasting Corporation radio broadcast, Hale recalled that they played for self-improvement, not for the entertainment of onlookers. Leacock, he remembers, was the better batsman.[2]

After 1895, Leacock, the young housemaster from Upper Canada College, spent most of his free time in Orillia with his mother, four sisters and three brothers. Hale remembered Mrs. Leacock as "a woman of charm, ability and character, adored by her children. Her wishes were to them commands and her commands law."[3] Agnes Leacock attended St. James Anglican Church, often accompanied by Stephen. The Hales were pillars of the parish. C.H. Hale, the lean young editor with only a partial high school education, was fast emerging as the canny chief booster and leading journalist of Leacock's new hometown. The friendship that developed between them was grounded in mutual respect and a sharing of certain values. Manly camaraderie had nothing to do with it. The friendship endured for half a century. Cricket was one shared interest (Leacock joined the Orillia Cricket Club early in the century), and sailing was another. Hale once told me that Leacock took a serious and proprietary interest in Orillia that seemed at odds with the caricaturing in *Sunshine Sketches*. Leacock knew and admired local achievers and characters, delighted in local gossip, joined in the town's social and sporting life and, when requested, volunteered his oratorical skills. He was among the first speakers to address the Orillia branch of the Canadian Club, founded by Hale in 1906. At the invitation of local Tories, he stumped Simcoe County in 1911 to urge rejection of Wilfrid Laurier's Reciprocity Treaty.

Hale and Leacock were lifelong Conservatives and fellow believers in a powerful British commonwealth. But on one issue they were light-years apart. Hale never accepted a drink from Stephen Leacock. Or from anyone else. He never uttered, however, a word of criticism about Leacock's well-known fondness for liquor. Even during Prohibition in the twenties and thirties, when booze binges at The Old Brewery Bay were whispered about on Orillia street corners, he remained silent. In Hale's moral universe, there were only responsible drinkers and hopeless drunks. Royalty, nobility and aristocracy, and men of genius and solid achievement such as Stephen Leacock and Sir John A. Macdonald, were responsible drinkers. The rest of indulging humankind, especially the working classes, were hopeless drunks, and no effort was to be spared to keep them out of the clutches of the booze barons.

In the first decade of the twentieth century, the *Packet* reported the comings and goings, the new books and lecture tours of Orillia's increasingly famous summer resident. In return, Leacock made sure that the *Packet* got its share of scoops. Regular dispatches reached the paper from Leacock's 1907 world tour. On 16 April the newspaper reported, "During his stay in England, Professor Stephen Leacock was the guest of Rudyard Kipling. The poet of Imperialism presented the new prophet of the movement with a pipe, as a remembrance of his visit."

The *Packet* never wavered in its admiration of Leacock's gifts and never underplayed the importance of his Orillia connection. The humorist responded to all the attention by passing along his comments, opinions and judgments, addressed invariably to "The Editor of the *Newspacket*, Orillia." Some of these were published but generally they were intended for the private amusement of C.H. Hale. In the spring of 1910 Leacock sent Hale a typewritten letter from Montreal, asking him to try to find a summer tenant for the Old Brewery Bay property. The professor wanted to go to England on publishing business. The rent would be a reasonable forty-five dollars. As his agent, Hale was to get five dollars. Leacock reasoned that advertising would cost nothing, since Hale owned the paper.

The *Packet* did not get every Leacock scoop. During the spring and summer of 1908 it made no mention of the professor's purchase of the Brewery Bay property on 15 April. The Friday 16 April edition notes only: "Dr. Stephen B. Leacock arrived in town yesterday and will spend the summer in Orillia. His friends here were glad to greet him after his trip around the world."

Leacock's name appears in four more editions of the paper in the following five months; none of them identify him as the owner of a substantial piece of property in Orillia. It was a rare slip-up for newshound C.H. Hale.

Stephen Leacock's death on 28 March 1944 was marked by editorial tributes across the world. The *Packet's* read:

> He was English born and spent a large part of his working life in Montreal, but Ontario nurtured him in his boyhood and gave him his education and it was to his favourite haunt on the shores of Lake Couchiching that he returned for most of each year for the evening of his days. But his loss will be deplored by a much wider public than the people of

Ontario, and in many corners of the world there will be mourning of the death of a man who during some of the most troubled decades in history made a steady contribution to the greater gaiety of mankind. Leacock was something more that a writer of great merit. He was one of the most versatile personalities of his time and he was a national even an international character. It was as a writer of humorous essays and sketches that he gained world-wide fame and his talent in that field probably reached its finest flower in "Sunshine Sketches Of A Little Town," in which he immortalized in a kindly vein of whimsical humour the daily ongoings in a small Ontario town adjacent to his boyhood's home. He gave free play to his wit and humour over a wide range of subjects and in his writings lost no opportunity to wage war upon arrogant pretensions, pomposity and humbug of all kinds. Yet his pen was never malicious and he had the capacity for making the victims of his wit laugh at themselves. The whole Canadian nation will be poorer by his loss. But the saddest mourners in it will be the wide circle of friends of both sexes in all ranks of society whose affection and admiration he had won. His wit made him welcome and an outstanding figure in any company, but what endeared him more to his friends was his charm of manner and his innate kindliness of heart. Fortunately he has left to the world and his friends the rich legacy of his diversified writings, which long will be read by discerning people, able to appreciate a happy combination of wit and wisdom. They will serve to keep green the memory of a great writer, a true Canadian and a loveable man.[4]

Robertson Davies also paid his respects the week of Leacock's passing, with a touch of wry prophecy:

Hector Charlesworth writes today that the people of Orillia never forgave Stephen Leacock for making mild fun of them in *Sunshine Sketches of a Little Town*. Ah, but wait a few years until Leacock's fame has spread and tourists begin to crowd Orillia. Then we shall see Ye Olde Leacock Bunne and Cake Shoppe, Ye Leacock Inne, and Bus Tours of lovely Leacockland suddenly spring up where indifference and resentment reigned before. A favorite maxim of commercial

life is: Never let personal feeling interfere with the exploitation of the Great Dead.[5]

Tribute, not exploitation, was on Hale's mind when he launched his last
and most ambitious Orillia campaign just days after Leacock's death. Letters
went out and phone calls were made in the time-tested manner, to assemble
key people. On 21 June at the Orillia Public Library he presided over the
birth of the Stephen Leacock Memorial Committee, composed of a half-
dozen Orillians like himself who had known the celebrated humorist as
friend or kindly host. Letters went out to native sons and daughters who had
made their mark and who could help publicize the campaign. Provincial treasurer Leslie M. Frost got one. So did the vice-president of Maclean Hunter,
Floyd Chalmers. Chalmers had spent his boyhood years in Orillia. Elizabeth
Wyn Wood, a renowned Orillia-born sculptor, was another recipient.
Leacock's literary and academic associates in Toronto and Montreal were can-
vassed. They all pledged support. The committee adopted three memorial
projects. A Leacock collection – books, letters and other memorabilia –
would be assembled at the Orillia Public Library. Elizabeth Wyn Wood
would be commissioned to create a Leacock portrait bust. And the Stephen
Leacock medal would be struck, for annual presentation to the author of the
best book of humour published in Canada. Enthusiasts in and out of Orillia
were invited to contribute to a $1500 fund to bring all this to fruition. The
goal was reached in a matter of months. Every industrial firm and commercial enterprise in Orillia gave. So did doctors and dentists and lawyers and
ordinary citizens. Orillia Town Council pledged a hundred dollars.
Donations came from corporation presidents who studied under Stephen
Leacock at McGill, from publishers who had earned high profits from his
works and from contemporary Canadian writers. And books arrived along
with cash. Rare editions of Leacock works were donated by American and
British publishers and libraries across the country.[6]

All three goals were met. The Leacock Medal for Humour, created by
Emanuel Hahn (the husband of Elizabeth Wyn Wood and designer of the
Canadian ten-cent and twenty-five coins), was presented for the first time on
Friday 13 June 1947 to Harry L. Symons, author of *Ojibway Melody*. And
the Leacock bust was unveiled on 15 September 1951 by Orillia-born
Premier Leslie Frost, in a corner of the Orillia Public Library where the
Leacock collection was housed.

Harry Symons did not receive his Leacock medal at the first award dinner, held at Orillia's Orchard Point Inn. He received an empty box! Hahn's
inspired design – Leacock profile on one side, and Mariposa's beaming sun
and hovering mosquitoes on the other – had not yet been cast. Symons's

mock indignation triggered gales of laughter, as did the remarks of everyone else on the program: George Leacock, Stephen's beloved brother, who was regarded by his siblings as the most humorous of the children; B.K. Sandwell, the *Saturday Night* editor who had serialized *Sunshine Sketches* in a Montreal paper thirty-seven years earlier; *Globe and Mail* critic William Arthur Deacon; Louis Blake Duff, a Welland, Ontario, historian and publisher, who was listed on the program as a humorist; and, of course, C.H. Hale. Once more he had proven to be the catalyst. What was begun that night, a melange of unbridled merriment and serious literary intent known as the Leacock Medal Dinner, has continued until the present day.

I was there that night, a nineteen-year-old radio reporter freshly arrived from Toronto at Orillia's CFOR. My first major assignment for my new employer was to record interviews after dinner, on direct-to-disk 78 RPM for a Sunday-morning broadcast special. In my resume I had dared to describe myself as a seasoned interviewer. During the preceding year in Toronto I had interviewed scores of personalities though never once with a microphone. I took notes, and the notes were worked into written questions for John Aylesworth, the host of a CBC radio show called "High Newsreel." I arrived, petrified, at the Leacock Medal Dinner, certain my lie would soon be revealed. But something remarkable happened. The dinner was so madcap, so roaringly and spontaneously funny, that my inhibitions melted away. There had never been anything like this before in my young life, or in the lives of anyone else present. I resolved there and then to be part of this movement, if I settled down in Orillia. The interviews I knocked off after dinner were amazingly free of "uhs" and "ahs" and the program director lauded the Sunday show. Several of the recordings I made that long-ago night are among the prized souvenirs of my career.

There was much to like about Orillia for a city-bred teenager in 1947, not least of all a radio station that encouraged creativity. I settled in as a boarder at 184 West Street North. My landlady, Lottie Mae Halloran, was as memorable an Orillia character as any sketched by Leacock. At the radio station my duties expanded. I was named farm editor, a logical appointment for someone born and raised in a Toronto suburb. And I filled Friday night and weekend on-air shifts doing passable imitations of Byng Whittaker and Elwood Glover, the reigning monarchs among Canadian DJs. For the balance of the week I wrote spots, endless variations of sixty-second commercial messages that began "Hey Mr. Farmer ..." or "Did you know ..."

My curiosity about Leacock's Orillia/Mariposa had been roused at the dinner but information about Leacock and his home was hard to come by. People talked of a Leacock estate somewhere along the lakefront, an eerie mansion that no one went near. They said it was a place closely guarded by

Stephen Leacock Jr., whose eccentric ways matched those of his late father.

Of the progress of the Leacock Memorial Committee I knew even less. The *Packet* regularly reported on its activities, but between the *Packet and Times* (the official name of the paper after a 1925 amalgamation with *The Times*) and CFOR a no man's land existed. It was *Packet* policy never to mention the radio station, not because of commercial rivalry but because the editor looked on commercial radio as a cultural wasteland. It would have been unseemly and unpolitical for a CFOR reporter to approach C.H. Hale, an Orillia legend, and express an interest in Leacock.

Enter Henry Janes.

Chapter Three

SAVING THE LEACOCK HOME, 1949

The Orillia-born son of Leacock crony Charlie Janes and a godson of the humorist, Henry Janes had studied economics under Leacock at McGill and worked for the professor, briefly, before the Second World War. In 1949 he owned and operated Public Relations Services Ltd. of Toronto, a firm that specialized in consumer surveys. That spring Stephen Leacock Jr. agreed to lease his father's estate to him for the balance of the year and consider an offer to purchase. As the weeks passed, the Orillia papers contained details of Henry Janes's hopes and plans for the property.

The price for the home and 28.8 acres of property would be $50,000. In an article in the Orillia *News-Letter* Janes spoke of the imminent launching of the "Stephen Leacock Foundation" by a "small group of McGill graduates and other Leacock admirers." The Foundation would solicit donations and grants from government, industry, other foundations and individuals to buy the home and "develop it." If that did not work there was also the possibility of the "formation of a private company to purchase the property and carry it on as a high class commercial venture."[1] He did not elaborate on what he meant by development or venture. That Janes had the approval of young Stevie Leacock in all this is certain. Stephen Jr. was a regular contributor to the *News-Letter* and a buddy of its editor, Bill Curran. In February Janes spoke to the Orillia Y's Men's Club on Leacock's career and philosophy. His final paragraph revealed his hopes for The Old Brewery Bay:

> But Stephen Leacock was a great teacher of the public, a great humanitarian. The principles of human progress and social reform which he wrote about so well are needed today more than ever. I believe, and fortunately more and more people are agreeing with me that his Orillia home should be maintained as a research centre, dealing with the subject to which he devoted so much of his life and work – human progress.[2]

Janes was not the first to propose a public use for the Leacock home. Robert Burrows, an Orillia-born Bell Telephone executive in the mid-1940s, had earlier suggested to Hale and the newly formed Memorial Committee that the home be acquired as a literary memorial. The committee liked the thought but could do little about it. The property was not on the market, and no government or foundation or individual had expressed interest. Moreover, the committee was spending all its energies and funds meeting its three original objectives.

I had no qualms about meeting Henry Janes, as I had about encountering Hale. Fate smiled on me, in fact. Henry's wife, Phyllis, a well-known artist, was a friend of my mother's. Both hailed from Alliston. My mother insisted that I make myself known to Henry and Phyllis and pass on her greetings. Accordingly, I called Janes one day in early June and he insisted that I come out to The Old Brewery Bay the following afternoon. It was not the Alliston connection alone that initiated our friendship. I was a member of the media and stroking the media was Henry's specialty. So, on a warm afternoon in June 1949, I finally set eyes on the Leacock home. It was enchantment at first sight. There were shattered windows, sagging shutters, a roof that leaked, weed-choked lawns and gardens, and mustiness, decay and neglect everywhere. The beautiful contours of Leacock's dream house, however, were still intact. It took only a little imagination to see what some fresh paint and a good scrub-down could accomplish. The Janeses were perfect hosts. I was welcomed with a pitcher of beer, served on the front verandah. We sat on wooden kitchen chairs overlooking the bay. The mood was mellow. Henry, genial and gentle-voiced, recalled happy times at this very spot, talking of Leacock as a father figure and of what he thought the great man would want to see done with his beloved home. To my astonishment, he asked my opinion. And I agreed that the home had to be saved, restored and opened to Leacock's vast public either as a seminar centre, as Janes urged, or as a museum, as I preferred.

In that heady summer of 1949 there was a change at The Old Brewery Bay. Led by O. Garnet Smith, the long-serving secretary of the Orillia Board of Trade, a band of volunteers – mostly businessmen – mowed the lawns, tamed the weeds and helped the Janeses clear cobwebs, dust and debris from the home and boathouse. Before the summer's work was under way, Janes had gone national with his plans and by mid-June could boast of impressive moral support. Graham Towers, the governor of the Bank of Canada, wrote, "I am most interested to read of your proposal to preserve the Stephen Leacock estate as a special point of interest in the Orillia district. Certainly a figure of Mr. Leacock's stature in Canadian letters deserves some tangible memorial."[3] From George A. Martin, president of the Canadian Association of Tourist and Publicity Bureaus, came congratulations and a promise of co-operation:

> Your desire to have the Orillia home of Stephen Leacock preserved as a possible literary centre and historical spot is one with which I heartily agree ... Our Association is most anxious to have historical landmarks preserved ... I am quite sure the Orillia home where he wrote so many of his books can be made into an historical centre which will become an increasing attraction with the passing years.[4]

In mid-August, reporter Herbert Macdonald of the *Montreal Standard Weekend Magazine* arrived to prepare a major story on the Janeses' efforts. He quickly fell under Henry's sway. The photo story carried in the 9 October 1949 issue of the nationally distributed supplement was mass media exposure of the sort public relations people kill for. The Leacock feature ran to four pages and included eight pictures. Even I appear in one of them, at Henry Janes's side, gleaning through Leacock lecture posters in a corner of the billiard room. Other photographs show teenagers from nearby Fern Cottage Resort cleaning up the boathouse; Phyllis Janes and her friend Verna McComb of Toronto sorting through books in the library; and the Board of Trade volunteers, led by O. Garnet Smith, in the area south of the sun porch, taking direction from Bill Jones, Leacock's long-time gardener.

The photographs are charming, if a bit stiff. The text accompanying them, however, is anything but charming. Macdonald is aghast at the apathy Canadians show towards their literary heritage and cites the deterioration of the Leacock home as a flagrant example: "Vandals had wintered in the house, in the years before the Janes arrival," he wrote. "The silver and china and some furniture were stolen. The doors and windows were broken. The bookshelves, groaning with first editions and some 16th century bindings were dumped on the floors. The boathouse rotted and slipped down on one corner like a tired old man. The roof leaked and winter froze the water to ice to encase the records of years of work and leave them rotting and hardly decipherable."[5] Macdonald continues:

> Out of desperation young Leacock turned the estate over to Henry Janes of Toronto ... He and his company entered into an arrangement to buy the property. Their efforts to form a Stephen Leacock Foundation were unsuccessful and they are going ahead on a private enterprise basis. There was no other course. It would have taken $50,000 to buy the estate and another $100,000 to maintain it.[6]

The story enraged Stephen Leacock Jr. In angry letters to the *Montreal Standard* and Orillia *Packet,* he denied any suggestion that he had been careless in protecting his father's home against the natural elements and vandals. In his letter to the *Standard* he complained:

> All this gives a picture of such extreme and woebegone dilapidation as to make the place appear uninhabitable, like a ghost mansion of the South. In answer I will merely say that I was living there myself in 1948 and not ashamed to be entertaining out-of-town guests, some of whom were from Montreal. As a matter of fact I also lived there every summer before that since my father's death in 1944 and left the place in the wintertime in the charge of tenant-caretakers. The property does need repairs and improvements and not a few of them (what large country estates do not from time to time?) but your gratuitous presentation of it as an unlived-in ruin – and thus you have presented it – is as false in fact as it is offensive in implication. For the impression given by what you have written is that the blame for this (mythical) collapse can be laid at the door of one person only – myself – the owner; and that it was through my apathy and carelessness and neglect that a priceless repository of Canadiana was abandoned to rot like a carcass on the desert. You are wrong.[7]

The letter to the *Packet's* editor drips with sarcasm and savagery, dismissing the notion that

> I myself have the brain of an aborigine and have lived at Old Brewery Bay since my father's death five and a half years ago

– scattering books and documents around like daisy petals and have no feeling for literature, art or history. It isn't so and I know you do not really think it of me, Mr. Editor – other things you may, and with pleasure, but not that I am not a member of the literary cognoscenti. I am and you know it. The second implication is that my derelict mansion – a meretricious phrase which I recommend to Mr. Janes for use in his future researches – has proved to be a treasure-trove of the memorabilia and personalia of my father. It hasn't. The manuscripts of my father's works – which are important – are in the library at McGill University, Montreal, and of other records there are very few of any real significance. I do not think my father realized that Mr. Janes would be wanting to collect them. I hope, Mr. Editor, that in the future we do not run into any more little contretemps or troubles such as this one. They can become bitter if carried too far.[8]

Janes's lease was cancelled, and talk of a Leacock foundation and a research/seminar centre at The Old Brewery Bay ended abruptly. If Herbert Macdonald had exaggerated the home's derelict state, based on Henry Janes's revelations and his own observations, young Stevie also toyed with the truth. Those of us who enjoyed the free run of the property in the summer of 1949 saw signs of gross negligence everywhere, and we were as pained and frustrated about it as Henry Janes or Herbert Macdonald. All too soon The Old Brewery Bay belonged again to the natural elements and vandals.

Chapter Four

THE LEACOCK CAUSE, 1949–1955

How the town of Orillia acquired the Leacock home is another Leacock story, riddled with the kind of ironies the humorist himself would have relished.

The story begins in October 1954, when a committee to acquire and restore the Leacock home was formed, just days before Hurricane Hazel slammed into southern Ontario. The committee's impact on Orillia was considerably less than the storm's. Hazel left flooded streets and basements, downed hydro and phone lines and scattered tree-limbs. The formation of the committee left only puzzled expressions, stifled yawns and plenty of skepticism.

Much had happened to me in the five years since I had first laid eyes on Leacock's summer home. I had married Eileen Giles and sired two sons. The radio station had moved to better studios and higher power. We were now grinding out network programming, most notably "The Dominion Barn Dance" on the CBC's Dominion network, a show on which a teenage Gordon Lightfoot made his broadcast debut one Saturday night in 1954 as a member of a barbershop quartet from Orillia District Collegiate.

The Leacock cause had been moving forward. In 1948, Paul Hiebert, creator of *Sarah Binks*, won the second Leacock medal. In 1949, Angeline Hango was awarded the third medal for *Truthfully Yours*. In 1950, it was Earle Birney's turn for *Turvey*. That was also the year the *Packet* finally recognized CFOR. I wrote most of the copy for a supplement the paper published in September when our power jumped to one thousand watts. Although the newspaper and radio station were still commercial rivals, they began to co-operate in a number of ways – pooling facilities to cover elections. The detente meant that I could approach C.H. Hale without feeling I was betraying my employers and when I finally met him, I was surprised at how informed the editor was on my enthusiasm for the Leacock home. The soul of courtesy and kindness, he spoke slowly and moved cautiously, reflecting his seventy-seven years. His mind was focused, however, and his capacity to organize was finely tuned. We found ourselves in complete agreement on the need to acquire and restore The Old Brewery Bay.

In September 1951, Orillia's then mayor Austin Cook proclaimed "Stephen Leacock Week," the first municipal honour ever accorded the humorist in his "Sunshine Town." Friday 14 September was the key day. That afternoon, at Hale's invitation, Premier Leslie Frost unveiled Elizabeth Wyn Wood's portrait bust of Leacock in a corner of the Orillia Public Library where an impressive collection of Leacock memorabilia was already in place. That night Vancouver writer Eric Nicol received the fifth Leacock medal for *The Roving I* at a dinner at Fern Cottage Resort. Louis Blake Duff traced the career of Stephen Leacock, and Hale disclosed the names of the real-life Orillians who inspired the characters in *Sunshine Sketches*. The editor was introduced for the first time as "Doctor" Hale. Earlier that summer the University of Toronto had conferred an honorary doctor of laws degree on him in recognition of a half-century of editorial excellence at the *Packet* and his unrivalled community leadership. The honour was instigated by Premier Frost. "Leacock Week," it goes without saying, was Hale's idea and received full-blown editorial support, of course, in the *Packet*. In an unsigned commentary Hale wrote:

> Beyond the efforts of the Leacock Memorial Committee and an agitation to preserve his home as a literary shrine, little has been done here. The Leacock Committee is to be congratulated on obtaining the bronze bust-portrait and for the annual award of the Leacock Medal for Humour.
>
> These things in themselves are splendid but we feel that even greater efforts should be made in the future. It is unlikely, however, that very much can be accomplished until Orillians realize that a very famous, very talented man of letters made this his home.[1]

During 1952 Hale continued his agitation to secure the Leacock home. That year the inner circle of the Leacock Memorial Committee – soon to be known as the Stephen Leacock Associates – was composed, literally, of the Orillia "associates" of the late humorist: farmer John Drinkwater and his family, Maude Ardagh and Marjorie Tudhope, members of two of Orillia's blue ribbon families who were frequent guests at the Old Brewery Bay in the 1920s and 1930s; lawyer Paul Copeland; the Hale brothers, C.H. and Russell; and a few others, aided and abetted by the dean of Canadian literary critics, the *Globe and Mail's* William Arthur Deacon, who summered in Orillia.[2] All were in their sixties and seventies. C.H Hale decided younger blood was needed and asked me to join the circle.

In November 1952 I entered my name as an aldermanic candidate for Orillia Town Council, with no particular agenda or special qualifications. There was no mention of Orillia's Leacock legacy in my platform speeches. Instead I would ad-lib some apple-pie sentiments, promise only to do my best and sit down. To my surprise, I topped the aldermanic polls, as I would do six more times in the next twelve years. A congratulatory note arrived from Hale, who knew that he had a Leacock ally on council. Elected mayor that same day was Wilbur M. Cramp, a master of political bombast, young Stevie's closest Orillia friend and a character who would figure prominently in the latter-day history of The Old Brewery Bay.

At the council's inaugural meeting on 4 January 1953 I was named chairman of the publicity and reception committee and handed an important assignment. Queen Elizabeth's coronation was scheduled for 3 June. Thanks in no small part to the unblinking imperialist views of the *Packet*, Orillia was arguably the most royal and most loyal of Canadian communities and so the town's celebration was to be extraordinary. Politicians and preachers were to play leading roles. There would be a colossal parade, sports and music in the park, ice cream for every youngster and a spectacular fireworks display – all of it in the Mariposa spirit. Of public entertainments in his mythical town Leacock wrote:

> – and amusements! Well, now! Lacrosse, baseball, excursions, dances, the Fireman's Ball every winter and the Catholic picnic every summer! and music – the town band in the park every Wednesday evening, and the Oddfellows Brass Band on the street every other Friday; the Mariposa Quartette, the Salvation Army – why, after a few months' residence you begin to realize that the place is a mere mad round of gaiety.[3]

All community leaders were consulted, Hale in particular. He was our idea man. At first his suggestions focused on Coronation activities, then ideas about Leacock crept into the notes he was sending us almost daily. One of them, in late May, was especially interesting. Why not prepare a leather-bound copy of *Sunshine Sketches of a Little Town* as the town's Coronation gift to the Queen? The thirty-six-member Coronation committee approved the idea unanimously. But time was short, and our budget was limited. The proposal was set aside, though not forgotten. At the committee's final meeting we discovered a surplus of funds. On 6 July, I proposed to town council we earmark $125 of the surplus for the Coronation copy of *Sunshine Sketches*. The motion lost, six votes opposed to only two in support. Immediately afterwards, Orillia was portrayed in a Toronto *Telegram* story, syndicated nation-wide, as insensitive to both its Leacock heritage and the monarchy.[4] I had argued that the book would be a fitting gift, something which could be read and enjoyed by all the members of the royal family. As far as I knew, ours was the only town in the Commonwealth to boast a writer of Leacock's stature. But Alderman Jack McDonald won the night, asserting that "it's nice to hobnob with royalty, but some flunky in Buckingham Palace will put the book away and I doubt if *Sunshine Sketches* would see much sunshine."[5]

I lost the battle but not the war. Six years later the Queen did receive her leather-bound copy of *Sunshine Sketches*, not at the front door of Buckingham Palace but in a ceremony at Orillia's Couchiching Beach Park. For the moment, Leacock devotees had been served notice that their cause cut little ice at Orillia City Hall.

A year and a half passed. October 1954 was a frantic month around CFOR. We were moving to new studios on West Street North. As program director I was responsible for the orderly transfer of studio equipment and thousands of recordings. During that hectic time, opportunity knocked at last, on the matter of public ownership of the Leacock home. Young Stevie had decided to offer The Old Brewery Bay to the town of Orillia for $50,000. The offer came in a letter to me from his lawyer, Griffith Bingham.[6] I passed the contents along to both Mayor John MacIsaac and Hale. Hale urged the mayor to call a public meeting and MacIsaac agreed. The meeting was set for an early October evening. Hale then telephoned members of the Leacock Associates and other sympathizers in Orillia and ordered them to show up; a big turnout would send a positive message to the town fathers. He also asked for proposals on strategies. I had a few, but I also had a problem. Our studio move was at a critical stage. I saw no chance of getting to the meeting that night. Hale then asked me to agree to act as chairman of a committee to acquire the home, if one was set up that night. I gave my consent, but insisted that I could serve for only three months.

I got to the meeting after all, but in its dying minutes. In grimy work clothes, I slipped into the council chambers just in time to learn a committee had indeed been formed, with myself as chairman. The mayor was present as were five members of council. Mayor MacIsaac, Reeve Mervyn Gardiner and

Deputy Reeve Tom Lambrick voiced support of the proposal. Aldermen Gordon Hammond and Victor Hall reserved judgment but not for long. When the purchase proposal was laid before council in a heated session on Monday 29 October, they spoke out vehemently. Hammond was incensed at the idea of the town considering an investment of $15,000 as a down payment on a rundown home when the same council had refused him $1000 for badly needed sidewalks in the west ward. Victor Hall, a retired tool and dye maker who had lived in Orillia since 1894, wondered why on earth we wanted to honour Leacock, a man he claimed to have seen weaving around town with his scarf dragging. Alderman Ken Curtis was in favour because a Leacock museum would attract tourists, but finance chairman Alderman Bill Brown said tourism was overrated as a mainstay of Orillia's economy. The town's real strength came from industrial development, he insisted. Besides, the town's solicitors had told him deficits from an Orillia-owned Leacock museum would be the responsibility of the town's already overburdened taxpayers. Letters of support for town ownership of the Leacock property, prompted by C.H. Hale, came from Louis Blake Duff, Gladstone Murray and William Arthur Deacon. Deputy Reeve Tom Lambrick asked, "Did they enclose any cheques?" The mayor lost his temper. "It's no laughing matter," he shot back. The reeve and deputy reeve, who had been supportive earlier, now favoured a public vote on the proposition, if anyone knew what the proposition really was. With matters getting out of hand, the mayor closed off the debate and referred the matter back to my committee.[7] Later I learned there was also a problem with protocol. My colleagues resented the offer coming to me alone, instead of to mayor and council. Two days after the rocky council session, Griffith Bingham sent me a letter to say Stephen Leacock Jr. was withdrawing his offer and would never again make his father's property available to the town of Orillia. We could blame council's cavalier attitude – Alderman Victor Hall's insulting comment particularly. The letter ended, however, with Bingham's personal thanks for our efforts and a hope the Leacock Home Committee would carry on. That surely meant we were being taken seriously by the one person who held the fate of the Leacock home in his hands.

Our committee continued to meet and to attract support. Before the end of 1954, the senior and junior Chambers of Commerce, the Orillia Historical Society, the Orillia Women's Institute, as well as both town newspapers and the radio station had pledged their backing. Charlie Greenwood, manager of Orillia's Geneva movie theatre and a skilled sign-maker on the side, joined the committee. Entirely on his own, he had lettered and erected a series of signs suggesting Orillia's principal Mariposa settings: Judge Pepperleigh's home (the Mundell Funeral Home on West Street North); Netley's Store and

Jeff Thorpe's Barber Shop, both on Mississaga Street East; and the "Beacon On The Hill" (St. James's Church) on Peter Street North. Although Hale attended few committee meetings, he stayed in almost daily touch through letters and phone calls. His strategies were unceasing. With the Orillia Town Council out of the picture, we would have to lobby other levels of government, he insisted, or try to line up a sympathetic purchaser. Hale had retired as editor of the *Packet* in 1951 but used his post as editor emeritus to promote Leacock awareness in Orillia and to ensure his successors at the paper, in particular James B. Lamb, the *Packet*'s general manager and chief editorialist, continued the paper's commitment to Orillia's Leacock heritage.

Lamb needed no coaxing. In his engaging autobiography, *Press Gang*, he relates how Orillia captivated him from the moment of his arrival in 1950 because to him it was still Mariposa. Nor did he miss the importance of C.H. Hale's unique role in community life. With admiration he described "C.H." as "a gangling, cantankerous teetotal Tory and his ramshackle newspaper, known to its Liberal detractors as *The Racket and Crimes!*"[8]

Lamb was an early recruit to the Leacock Home Committee and just as quickly became its friend and confidant, as full of enthusiasm and ideas for what was afoot as his revered predecessor at the paper. Soon after council rejected the opportunity to secure the Leacock home he wrote a biting editorial:

> Municipal councils are notoriously short-sighted in such matters and require the prodding of citizens of some breadth of vision. Certainly Orillia needs better sidewalks and will, in time, get them. But would anyone be so foolish as to argue that the Champlain monument be melted down for sidewalk material?[9]

An editorial on 15 February 1955 in the Orillia *News-Letter* takes much the same tack, concluding: "Orillians must show interest first before they can expect help from outsiders."

In July 1955 the estate was once more on the market, this time listed by Rideout Realty of Toronto and advertised in the *Globe and Mail.* The asking price was still $50,000. In a *Globe and Mail* feature on 28 July, Orillia correspondent Red Gordon dealt extensively with the intentions of our committee. Again we were talking about a Leacock foundation and a national fundraising drive. Shades of 1949 and Henry Janes! But this time there was no angry outburst from young Stevie.

Among prospective buyers shown through the home in July was Victor C. Wansbrough, executive director of the Canadian Metal Mining Association in Toronto. On 19 August 1955, the Toronto *Globe* and

Montreal *Gazette* announced that Wansbrough had bought the estate for $47,500 and intended to maintain it as "a national literary shrine." Wansbrough's background was impeccable: a close friend of the Leacock family, principal of Lower Canada College in Montreal when young Stevie was a student there, and a man of substantial means and aesthetic inclinations. In an article published in the *Gazette* in mid-September 1955 he recalled visiting Leacock's Orillia estate for the first time in July 1923, as a member of a touring lacrosse team from Oxford and Cambridge universities. Orillia was an important stop, for the town's teams were perennial champs. Leacock invited the visitors to his lakeside home for refreshments and a dance.

> It was a grand affair and a notable occasion. Joy was unconfined. The female youth and beauty of Orillia and environs graced the ball. There were strolls beside the lake on moon-flooded lawns. Party dresses glittered and shimmered amid the twinkling lights of the winking glow-worms and Chinese lanterns. There were – but enough! Monastic Oxford was never like this. When, in the exorable march of time the festivities came to a close we were sped back at the break of day across the waters on the Leacock launch with Captain Stephen at the helm. In the teeth of the boisterous wind his booming voice mingled nautical instruction, imprecations and snatches of song as boisterous as the wind itself![10]

The story recalls many accounts of similar festivities on Old Brewery Bay in the 1920s. The Leacocks were so pleased with the success of the ball that they invited the players back on Sunday for tea. Wansbrough continues:

> Stephen explained that he had a particularly bad day and that tea was not for him. Indeed the family was living under the shadow of a serious accident. Someone, in removing a block of ice from the ice-house, had dropped it on his foot and thereby incapacitated himself. In telling the story Stephen reached out a hand and removed from his conveniently adjacent Scotch-and-soda an ice cube which he cautiously dropped on his toe. He then announced that he was in no better shape than the wounded man and was therefore unable to discharge any responsibilities as host.
>
> As far as tea and buns were concerned, we were "on our own."[11]

In the preface to the *Gazette* article, Wansbrough makes clear why he did not buy the property as a summer home for his family. He wanted "to preserve the name and fame of Stephen Leacock."[12] The Leacock Home Committee was ecstatic. "Understanding Mr. Wansbrough's intentions," I told the *Globe and Mail* on 19 July, "we were indeed grateful." But what were his intentions? For the next four months we tried but failed to find out. Immediately after the story's appearance in the *Globe and Mail* the committee sent Wansbrough a letter detailing our history and hopes and asking for a meeting as soon as possible to see if the committee's mandate and his own plans were compatible. He replied, briefly and politely, adding nothing to what he had already told the newspaper and promising to sit down with us at some future, unspecified time. It was not the response we had hoped for. C.H. Hale invited him to the Leacock Medal Dinner in mid-November, to accept the gratitude of all Leacock devotees, in particular the Leacock Home Committee. He accepted, but at the last moment wired to say he could not attend. We paid our respects anyway. At the dinner at Fern Cottage Resort, honouring Robertson Davies for *Leaven of Malice*, I proposed a toast to Victor Wansbrough, in absentia, as the "saviour" of the Leacock home. The applause was prolonged.

On 30 November, two weeks later, Stephen Leacock Jr. informed the press that the deal with Victor Wansbrough was off. His purchase had not been a purchase at all, but only a lease and an option of buy. Young Stevie told the Orillia *News-Letter* that "an amicable settlement was reached with Mr. Wansbrough," whom he described as a friend of thirty years' standing.[13] Did this development mean the property was for sale again? Young Stevie would say only that he was settling in for the winter in the Toronto suburb of Willowdale and that he might take up residence in the spring at the housekeepers lodge at The Old Brewery Bay. And he added in an aside aimed at the Leacock Home Committee, "I appreciate the interest of Orillia friends in the deal but I've authorized no one to try to find another buyer or make a deal for me. This is a matter I consider strictly my business."[14]

By the autumn of 1955 we were well acquainted with young Stevie's erratic ways. In April of that same year, six months after he had ruled out the town of Orillia as a buyer of the estate, I had phoned to introduce myself and ask for an informal meeting. He was happy to oblige. Up until then I had seen him only at a distance; we had never been introduced. At the little lodge a few nights later he poured a large rye for me and an even larger one for himself, lit a cigar and invited my questions. His appearance was jarring. Scarcely five feet in height, he wore an overcoat that reached to the floor. Black uncut hair pushed towards his shoulders from beneath a black fedora. He wore horn-rimmed specs, circa 1930. Here was a man of forty looking for all the world like a mischievous boy who had swiped some adult clothes for a costume party. I asked him if the home was to be sold, as rumour had it, and how he felt about its conversion to a literary museum by either a local committee or an outside buyer. Instead of answering, he launched into a bitter denunciation of all things Orillian. He demolished the idea that *Sunshine Sketches* had been a labour of love for his father. Further, when he wrote the book, his father held Orillians in contempt for their ignorance and hypocrisy and grubby scheming! The book is a put-down, young Stevie declared, and not the portrayal of bucolic innocence people take it to be. It took me a while to realize that this outrageous behaviour was young Stevie's way. He would toss out outlandish notions, then listen, bemused, as responses were sputtered back. Our own debate raged back and forth that evening for an hour or more, I sputtering, Stevie replying with scholarly detachment and snippets of wisdom, but never forgetting to refill the glasses. Later I was to discover that Stevie was trying to mimic his father's style and language as the senior Leacock might have held court a generation earlier on this same shoreline. But there was little genuine similarity. His father may have been bitter at times, but there was always a core of deep compassion within him for mankind's follies and failures. For young Stevie there was only cynicism. Life at the little lodge was surreal. Young Stevie's companion that summer was a large uncombed dog of undetermined breed who kept sightseers at bay, dropped fur wherever he walked, and bedded down with his master when the lights went out at three or four in the morning. Then there were the piano interludes. Three times during my first visit Stevie moved from his armchair to the upright piano and began to play a melody of great passion and tenderness. It was lush and cloying and infinitely sad, building in intensity for forty bars before it ended abruptly. On that evening Stevie told me he was the composer and that he had a reason for abandoning the music at that particular point but would not tell me the reason. The music was totally at odds with his conversational cynicism. He played it with the panache of a concert performer. Before the summer ended I began to understand the sad song as a metaphor for the tragic life of its composer.

I came away from that first encounter convinced young Stevie would be part of the problem, not part of the solution, if ever we struck a deal for his father's home. At his invitation, I returned to the little lodge a half dozen times in the spring and summer of 1955 to talk about Orillia and Orillians, national politics and international affairs, social movements and a dozen more topics. It was always one-on-one, Stevie brilliant and bitter, dropping sarcasms like drops of acid, and I taking the politically correct high road. He always drank too much. On at least two occasions I guided him to his bed before departing into the night. I felt sorry for him, but he despised pity.

By June 1955 I knew Stevie well enough to gain access to the main house for the first time in six years. I explored the place several times and on one visit began to pick up and stash away items of importance scattered around the library and den. One such item was a torn file folder labelled "Letters From Damn Fools," which I stowed in an upstairs closet.

I used my budding friendship with Stevie to get Ralph Curry inside the Leacock home. Curry, thirty-one years of age, was the charming and effusive head of the Department of English at Georgetown College, Kentucky. He had devoted years to a doctoral study of Stephen Leacock and hoped that his dissertation could be turned into a popular biography. Curry arrived in Orillia in July 1955, anxious to talk to everyone who had known Leacock. We got together for coffee one morning and found ourselves in harmony on practically everything. What our movement lacked was a Ralph Curry, an academic expert on the man we were determined to honour, a scholar and skilled administrator to call on if and when the home was ours and a museum had to be organized. He was the right person at the right time. Moreover, he would be available when we needed him. Summer was his free season. Finally, his enthusiasm for the humorist was such that he probably would have paid for the privilege of establishing a Leacock museum at The Old Brewery Bay. I am not sure if all of this was obvious at our first meeting, but once a rapport was established, it did not take long for the committee to realize that he was our man.

When Curry came to town he expected to be made welcome at The Old Brewery Bay but found the gate barred. He asked if I could help. I could. A phone call to Stevie set up a meeting. The Kentucky professor impressed the younger Stephen Leacock with his southern manners and Kentucky drawl, but even more with his erudition. Stevie had been a university teacher himself, briefly, and he recognized a kindred soul. Curry's reward was unlimited access to the home and its unsorted treasures. I'll never forget Ralph's bug-eyed wonder on his first visit. He kept saying, "Golly! Golly!" over and over like a child on Christmas morning. He spent four and a half days poring over private papers no scholar had ever seen.[15] Before Curry left for Kentucky, we came to an understanding. He would be the committee's literary advisor. If we managed to purchase the home, we would consider him a prime candidate for curator. Beginning in September 1955, Ralph Curry was solidly in our circuit.

Simcoe County Land Registry Office

This Indenture

made in duplicate the *Fifteenth* day of *April* in the year of our Lord One thousand nine hundred and eight. In pursuance of the Act respecting Short Forms of Mortgages,

Between

Stephen Butler Leacock of the City of Montreal, in the Province of Quebec, Professor, hereinafter called the Mortgagor,

Of the First Part.

Beatrix Maude Leacock, wife of the said party of the first part,

Of the Second Part.

And,

Jane Agnes Thomson and Frances Augusta Bridal Thomson, Spinsters, both of the Town of Orillia, in the County of Simcoe Helen Mary Joy of the same place, Widow, and William Grant Law Clerk, Charlotte Georgina Evans Spinster, and Francis George Evans, Barrister, all of the Town of Orillia, executors of the last will of Frank Evans, deceased, hereinafter called the Mortgagees,

Of the Third Part.

Witnesseth that in consideration of Eight Hundred ——————— dollars of lawful money of Canada now paid by the said Mortgagees to the said Mortgagor (the receipt thereof is hereby by him acknowledged) **The** said Mortgagor **Doth Grant and Mortgage** unto the said Mortgagees their heirs executors, administrators and assigns forever

All and Singular that certain parcel, or tract of land and premises situate, lying and being in the Town of Orillia in the County of Simcoe, and Province of Ontario and being composed of part of the West half of Lot Number Ten, in the Sixth Concession of the Township of South Orillia and now forming part of the said Town, containing by admeasurement nineteen acres and seventy three, one hundredths of an acre, be the same, more or less, and which may be more particularly known and described as follows, that is to say: Commencing at the intersection of the Easterly limit of the allowance for road between concessions Five and six, with the Northerly limit of the Right of Way

The Old Brewery Bay mortgage, above and on following page. On 15 April 1908 Professor Leacock paid $1600 for 19.73 acres of land on the Old Brewery Bay; the sellers took back an $800 four-year mortgage.

of the Grand Trunk Railway Company of Canada, Thence South eighty one degrees, fifteen minutes East along said Northerly limit, twelve chains and two links; Thence North forty seven degrees, nineteen minutes, and thirty seconds East eleven chains and sixteen links, more or less, to the shore of Lake Couchiching, Thence North Easterly, Northerly, South Westerly, and North Westerly following the several courses and windings of said shore line thirty one chains and ninety links, more or less, to the South, Easterly limit of a certain property known as the Brewery property, Thence South twenty six degrees, thirty seven minutes, and thirty seconds West, along said limit, three chains and forty two links, to the South Westerly limit of said property, Thence North forty three degrees forty eight minutes and thirty seconds West, along said limit, three chains and ninety one links, to the Southerly limit of a certain lane known as Brewery Lane, Thence South Western along said limit of said lane, eleven chains and ninety six links, to the Easterly limit of the allowance for road between said Concessions five and six; thence South twenty five degrees, fifty eight minutes, and thirty seconds East, along said limit, one chain and seventy links, more or less, to the place of beginning.

And the said Beatrix Mauie Leacock wife of the said party of the first part, hereby bars her dower in the said lands.

Provided this **Mortgage to be Void** on payment of **Eight Hundred** —————————— dollars of lawful money of Canada with interest yearly at **five** per cent per annum as follows: Said principal money to become due and be repaid, in four years from the date of these presents. Together with interest, payable yearly at the rate aforesaid. Together with interest on all overdue principal and interest, at said rate. The first payment of interest to be made one year from the date of these presents.

and Taxes and performance of Statute Labour

Leacock Museum Archives

The first Leacock building on the bay shore grew from a 1908 "cook house."

Leacock Museum Archives

The summer of 1916 saw a major expansion of the Leacock cottage.

Tea on the deck, 1917. Stephen Leacock at left, Freddie Pellatt, Beatrix Leacock, and Mrs. May "Fitz" Shaw holding little Stevie.

Leacock's 1919 boathouse on eastern shore of Old Brewery Bay.

Stephen Leacocks, Senior and Junior, at Old Brewery Bay, 1917.

Little Stevie in his mother's arms at Old Brewery Bay, 1917.

Winter at The Old Brewery Bay, circa 1928. Leacock with young Stevie and neighbour Peggy Shaw.

Stephen Leacock in the mid-1920s, a passport photo.

Orillia House

Lumber Cost

Posts -- 100 @ $1.00 ----------- $100.00

hemlock at $40 a thousand

Sills	—	550
joists	—	4900
Studding	—	3069
Plates	—	830
floor (under)	—	1850
floor (upstairs under floor)	—	1300
rafters	—	1025
roof sheeting	—	2050

15,585 $623.400
40
$623.400

Hardwood flooring at $70   .850 / 70 / 59.500 $60.

Second class flooring at 50   { 1100 / 1300 / 2,400 / 5 / 120.00 } $120

                  for $903.

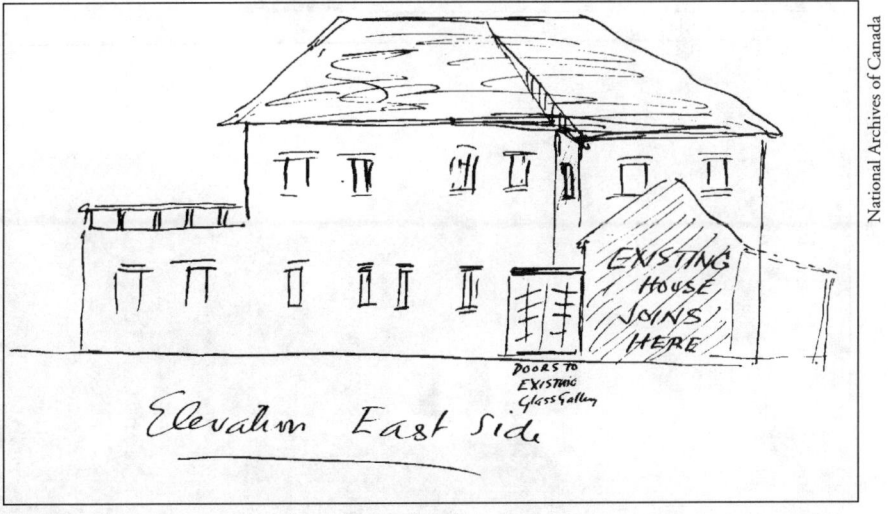

EXISTING HOUSE JOINS HERE

DOORS TO EXISTING Glass Gallery

Elevation East Side

In 1923 Leacock sketched an expanded summer home and estimated the cost. The scheme was abandoned as too expensive.

Leacock's dream home under construction, May 1928. Young Stevie poses before what will become the verandah.

A 1928 postcard view of The Old Brewery Bay.

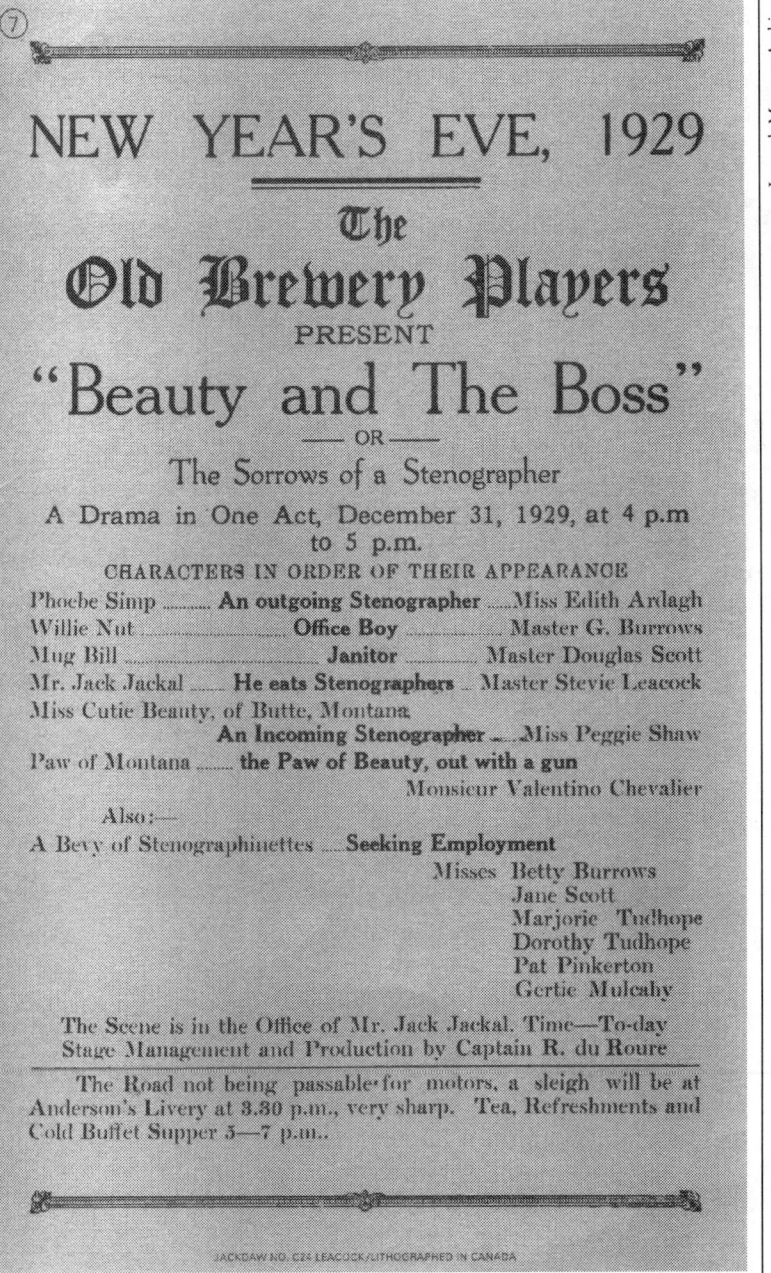

Home-made entertainment at The Old Brewery Bay, New Year's Eve, 1929.

Young Stevie by the living room fireplace, around 1940.

The Stephen Leacock Medal for Humour, designed by Emanuel Hahn and
presented each year but one since 1947.
Leacock Museum Archives

Reverse of Stephen Leacock Medal for Humour.
Leacock Museum Archives

Leacock Museum Archives

Head table guests at the first Leacock Medal Dinner, 13 June 1947. Left to right: William Arthur Deacon, C.H. Hale, Harry Symons (medal winner), Paul Copeland (chairman), B.K. Sandwell and George Leacock.

Leacock Museum Archives

The Old Brewery Bay belonged to vandals and the elements after Leacock's death in 1944.

Leacock Museum Archives

The sun porch at The Old Brewery Bay lay in ruins in the mid-1950s.

Montreal Standard Weekend Magazine, 8 October 1949

Toronto publicist Henry Janes leased The Old Brewery Bay in the summer of 1949. Poring over lecture posters in the billiard room are Glenna Leigh, Orillia reporter, Henry Janes and the author.

Mining executive Victor Wansbrough took an option on The Old Brewery Bay in 1955 but allowed it to lapse.

26 March 1957 – Orillia buys the Leacock home! Posed in mayor's office, left to right: Deputy Reeve Bill Greer, Mayor Wilbur M. Cramp, Alderman J.A. "Pete" McGarvey, Louis W. Ruby and solicitor Griffith Bingham.

James B. Lamb of the *Packet and Times* wrote an editorial that loosened Ottawa's purse strings.

Guests gather for Opening Day, 5 July 1958. Left to right: P.B. (Doc) Rynard, MP; Louis W. Ruby; Mrs. Marie Ruby; Premier Leslie M. Frost; Gordon E. Smith (who transported VIPs in his fleet of antique autos); and Hon. Alvin Hamilton.

Orillia Packet and Times

C.H. Hale, godfather of the Leacock home campaign, cuts the ribbon, 5 July 1958.

Orillia Packet and Times

The Hon. Alvin Hamilton, our angel from Ottawa, turns golden key to open The Old Brewery Bay, 5 July 1958.

Stephen Leacock's Orillia home on the south shore of Lake Couchiching in the Town of Orillia, built in 1927, purchased by the Town of Orillia, April 1957, restored by the Orillia Parks Board and the Stephen Leacock Memorial Home Board, 1957-1958.

OFFICIAL OPENING and DEDICATION OF THE

Stephen Leacock Memorial Home

"THE OLD BREWERY BAY"

ORILLIA, ONTARIO

Saturday, July 5, 1958, at 2 p.m.

A dream comes true – 5 July 1958.

Our first special guest, Canadian-born author/editor Thomas Costain, with the author, 4 September 1958.

Photo by Bruce Reed, McGarvey collection

Orillia *Packet and Times*

(Above) Bas Mason, an unheralded hero of The Old Brewery Bay. The *Telegram*'s dynamic but camera-shy promotion man at the "Meet the Authors" Dinner, 14 April 1959, escorting Maude Morrison Stone, oldest of sixty authors present.

Columnist Wessely Hicks of the Toronto *Telegram*, a mayor of Mariposa and organizer of the "Meet the Authors" Dinner to restore the Leacock sun porch.

James Pauk

4 July 1959: The Queen receives a copy of *Sunshine Sketches* from eight-year-old Peter McGarvey during an Orillia visit. Six years before, town councillors turned down a proposal to send the book to Buckingham Palace as a Coronation gift.

Orillia Packet and Times

11 June 1960: A young Pierre Berton wins Leacock Medal for Humour for *Just Add Water and Stir*. To the author's left is William Arthur Deacon.

Orillia Packet and Times

Chief Justice Patrick Kerwin comes calling, July 1958. Ralph Curry on the left, the author on the right.

Canada's foremost character actor, John Drainie (left), played a leading role in promoting Leacock. Here he is shown with Ralph Curry on lawn at The Old Brewery Bay, August 1957.

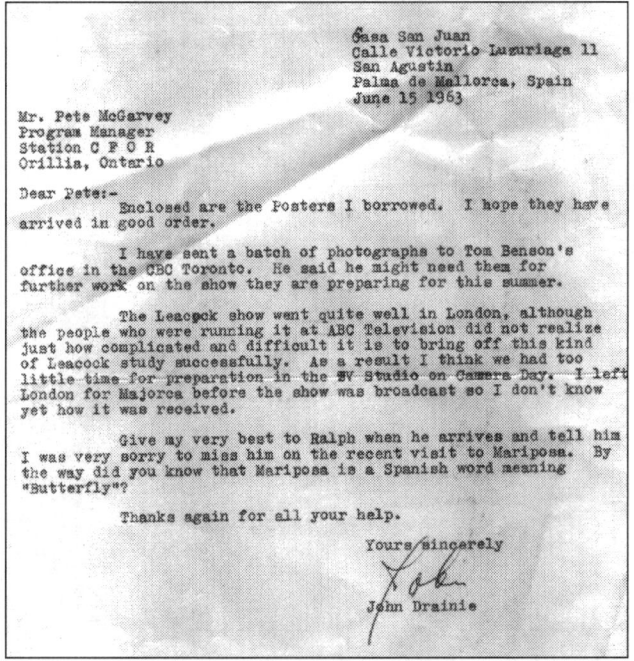

Casa San Juan
Calle Victorio Luzuriaga 11
San Agustin
Palma de Mallorca, Spain
June 15 1963

Mr. Pete McGarvey
Program Manager
Station C F O R
Orillia, Ontario

Dear Pete:-
        Enclosed are the Posters I borrowed. I hope they have arrived in good order.

        I have sent a batch of photographs to Tom Benson's office in the CBC Toronto. He said he might need them for further work on the show they are preparing for this summer.

        The Leacock show went quite well in London, although the people who were running it at ABC Television did not realize just how complicated and difficult it is to bring off this kind of Leacock study successfully. As a result I think we had too little time for preparation in the TV Studio on Camera Day. I left London for Majorca before the show was broadcast so I don't know yet how it was received.

        Give my very best to Ralph when he arrives and tell him I was very sorry to miss him on the recent visit to Mariposa. By the way did you know that Mariposa is a Spanish word meaning "Butterfly"?

        Thanks again for all your help.

                        Yours sincerely

                        John Drainie

John Drainie pursued his love for Leacock to the end of his life. A 1963 letter from Spain describes a one-man show in London.

McGarvey collection

Orillia *Packet and Times*

Famed comedian Frank Shuster makes the pilgrimage to The Old Brewery Bay, 21 July 1958.

McGarvey collection

Premier Leslie Frost honours his mentor, C.H. Hale, on his eighty-fifth birthday. A portrait bust of the aged editor, created by Elizabeth Wyn Wood, is unveiled. Author stands between Frost and Hale.

"Sunshine Sketches of a Little Town," the handwritten manuscript, is presented to the Leacock Museum, 26 August 1966. From left to right: Stephen Franklin, representing Montreal Standard Publishing; Barbara Nimmo; and Ralph Curry.

Leacock Museum Archives

Last run of "The Train to Mariposa" (see final chapter of *Sunshine Sketches of a Little Town*), 21 June 1958. The author met the engineer and crew at the station.

Orillia *Packet and Times*

Entranceway from the Atherley Road to The Old Brewery Bay, 1959.

Leacock Museum Archives

The Leacock home's original gift shop and guide centre, a retired city transit bus, sinking ever deeper in the mud.

Jay Cody collection

1980: Canada's vice-regal couple visit The Old Brewery Bay. Governor General Edward Schreyer and Lily Schreyer (centre) with Jay and Joan Cody.

Jay Cody collection

Opposition Leader – soon to be prime minister – Jean Chrétien poses with curator Jay Cody at Leacock home, August 1992.

The venerable mayor of Mariposa, Harry J. Boyle, at Winner's Announcement Party, May 1985. Author on left.

Daphne Mainprize, curator of the Stephen Leacock Museum (1994–).

Parks Canada

26 June 1994: The Old Brewery Bay is proclaimed a National Historic Site. At mike, Thomas Symons, chairman of the National Historic Sites and Monuments Board, son of Harry Symons, winner of the first Leacock Medal for Humour.

The long-awaited Leacock Resource Centre, Swanmore Hall, opened June 1994.

Chapter Five

LOU RUBY STRIKES A DEAL, 1956

The year 1956 began with a boost for Stephen Leacock in Orillia. In late January, developer Hugh Grant opened the Stephen Leacock Hotel and Pavilion at the edge of Couchiching Beach Park. George Leacock was the guest of honour. "The Leacocks have closed many a hotel in their time," he quipped, "this is the first time we've opened one!" Later he put to rest a rumour that his celebrated brother was overly fond of Scotch. "He was no more fond of Scotch than he was of rye, rum, gin or vodka," he explained.

Wessely Hicks, a Toronto *Telegram* columnist who looked and wrote like Robert Benchley, attended the luncheon and later toured the home at The Old Brewery Bay. It was a depressing sight:

> Inside, the house was damp and clammy and cold as ingratitude. There is little furniture left now. The windows are streaked and floors are littered and there's the smell of an old house dying ... In cardboard cartons there are scores of Leacock manuscripts. He wrote long-hand in a tall and angular script on unlined paper and there are no corrections. The words seemed to have flowed thickly and steadily like warm milk.[1]

Stephen Leacock Jr. had a change of heart soon after disclosing his winter plans to *News-Letter* editor Bill Curran in the autumn of 1955. He listed the estate with A.E. Lepage in Toronto – again for $50,000 – and on 12 March

1956 the property had a new owner. This time it was a genuine transaction, no catches, hitches or options. The buyer was Louis W. Ruby, Toronto publisher, property developer and horseman. The price was $45,000. He paid $17,000 down and young Stevie took back a mortgage for $27,500.

Ruby's contribution to Canadian letters to that date had been *Flash Magazine*, Toronto's 1956 equivalent of today's *National Enquirer*. Canada's first scandal sheet, it made him a fortune, which he invested in property and horses. He was a canny, plain-spoken, self-taught entrepreneur who advanced in the world from back-pack pedlar in Algonquin Park to real estate mogul in Toronto by dint of hard work and a sure instinct for business opportunity. Although he had only the vaguest notion of Stephen Leacock's prominence, he knew a property bargain when he saw one.

Immediately after the purchase was announced, I telephoned him and then hurried to Toronto when he expressed interest in talking to me about the fate of Leacock's summer home. His newspaper office was a set of rooms at 56 Adelaide Street East, piled high with coffee cups, back copies of his paper and other debris generated by a bustling editorial venture. Ruby called his business John Blunt Publications. Blunt was exactly the operative word for the proprietor. "What are you going to do with the home?" I asked. "I dunno," he replied, "maybe tear it down. You could place two or three good-sized houses on that ridge." My blood froze. I pressed the case for preservation, for making a deal with our committee, for anything but demolition. By the time I left he had agreed to think about it. We met twice more before the end of April. By the time of our second meeting, Ruby was a convert to saving the Leacock home. He had been "talked to" by some of his media cronies, including broadcaster Byng Whittaker, who convinced him that Stephen Leacock was the genuine article and that he would be burned at the stake if he even thought of demolishing Leacock's home. Whittaker and others, he added, also were very interested in what might be in the home, manuscripts, letters, business records, photographs, etc. They'd even suggested that such materials were likely worth much more than all the acreage at Old Brewery Bay. They were right and I was worried. I called on Whittaker, an old friend, and begged him to see things from the committee's side. In my third meeting in Toronto I struck a deal with Lou Ruby, a remarkably generous deal. He was giving us a year to raise $25,000 to buy the home along with an adjoining acre of land for parking – 1.4 acres in all. If we succeeded he would turn over the entire contents of the house, on which he had taken out an option, as a personal gift. He asked for no deposit and gave us free run of the property for the summer to plan our restoration and conduct an inventory. I left his office with a letter setting out the terms of our agreement.

The sun burst through at last. The committee had a financial target that seemed ridiculously modest after years of considering goals of $50,000 and $75,000.

By the time of my first meeting with Ruby in March 1956 support for the preservation of the Leacock home was gathering momentum. William Arthur Deacon kept his readers well informed on all that was happening. The Leacock Medal Dinners in Orillia also were attracting Canada-wide attention. And the Canadian Broadcasting Corporation was devoting much radio and television time to Leacock features, making use of the talents of John Drainie. Canada's leading character actor, he worshipped Leacock and considered the preservation of The Old Brewery Bay something of a sacred cause. The home became a backdrop for several of his television adaptations of Leacock's works. Until his death on 30 October 1966, at the age of fifty, John Drainie was the definitive Stephen Leacock on stage, radio and television. He and his wife Claire often came to Orillia, made many friends, and used their influence to persuade others at the CBC and the theatrical community to become involved. By the mid-1950s a new generation of readers was also discovering Leacock. Later in the decade, McClelland and Stewart satisfied this demand with a reissue of Leacock classics in the newly established New Canadian Library.

With this kind of national sympathy and a property option in hand, the committee was certain of success the next time it appealed to Orillia's town fathers. Surely by now council would recognize the urgency of preserving a priceless piece of Canadiana within the community. And not for cultural reasons alone. There was money to be made: a Leacock museum in Orillia would be the perfect vehicle to advertise and market the town's identity as Mariposa and develop the tourist economy. But for the third time in four years my trust in my fellow councillors was shattered. A motion in April 1956 that Orillia buy the Leacock home from Lou Ruby for $25,000 failed. This time there were no headline-catching aldermanic sneers. It was simply a matter of money and budget priorities. The merits of the proposition were never contested. Several councillors voted for the motion, but not enough of them to swing the vote. For the committee it was a hard blow. Should we continue to push town council, hoping for a change of heart? Or should we take our case to higher governments as part of a national campaign?

As usual, Hale was full of ideas. He wrote to Premier Frost, asking the province to consider buying the home as a provincial historic site or at the very least pledging some funds towards the purchase if the Orillia Town Council would do the same. The response was cordial but non-committal. The premier passed the inquiry to the Department of Lands and Forests (Parks Department) and to the provincial Archeological and Historic Sites Board, at that time under the chairmanship of William Cranston of Midland.

In the end the answer was "no" from both bodies. W.B. Greenwood, chief of the Division of Parks, wrote in early September 1956 that his office handled only recreational developments. He suggested that Orillia might take on the project by itself or in partnership with Simcoe County.[2] From the Archeological and Historic Sites Board came appreciation for our efforts but no cash. Why did we get the cold shoulder from Queen's Park at such a crucial moment? If Frost was as proud of his Orillia roots as he claimed to be, and constantly attentive to Hale's counsel, why would he turn a deaf ear? Was the reason an ancient feud between the Leacocks and the Frosts? One of Frost's biographers hinted to me in Lindsay many years later that the teetotalling Presbyterian Frosts of Canice Street may have harboured animosity towards their Anglican neighbours, the Leacocks, who drank. Or was Bill Cranston the obstacle?

While the provincial government could not find $25,000 dollars to buy the Leacock home in 1956, within a few years it was appropriating hundreds of thousands of dollars to convert a site beside the Wye River, outside Midland, into Ste-Marie-Among-the-Hurons, and later, large sums to restore Fort Penetanguishine, in the community adjoining Midland. Both projects were promoted at Queen's Park by Cranston and were carried out under his general direction as chairman of the Huronia Historic Sites Board. Over the years, Cranston made it clear that he did not consider Orillia and the surrounding area part of Huronia, even though historians did. Huronia is defined as the region between Lake Couchiching and Lake Huron occupied by the Huron nation in the seventeenth century. In 1961, he refused financial assistance to an archaeological dig at Cahiague, eight kilometres west of Orillia, being carried out by Norman Emerson of the University of Toronto. Cahiague was the largest of all Huron settlements, comprising more than a hundred longhouses. The only financial assistance given to Emerson and his crew came from the Orillia Chamber of Commerce. We felt The Old Brewery Bay of the twentieth century was as deserving of Huronia Sites grant money as Fort Penetanguishine of the nineteenth century. But we received not a dime.

If not to the Ontario government, where could the Leacock Home Committee look for help? By mid-1956, we began a systematic canvass of corporate and private foundations, paying particular attention to those offering funds for artistic or literary projects. It was slow work, but we had more help now. Ralph Curry was unable to come north but offered suggestions in frequent letters. Grace Crooks, Orillia's new chief librarian, was recruited by the Leacock Home Committee to succeed Mary Sheridan, her predecessor at the library and a charter member of the committee. Warm and gracious, Grace Crooks was an accomplished writer with a deep appreciation of

Leacock. She would prove an invaluable addition to our circle.

Summer turned into autumn. With a closing date on Ruby's offer approaching, we had no money in the bank and no commitments from governments or foundations. I called Ruby with the bad news. There seemed little chance we could meet our deadline of early 1957. Also, his option to buy the contents of the home expired at the end of 1956. He was disappointed but understanding. "Don't worry," he said, "I'm not going to do anything rash."

Nothing had changed by mid-November and nomination night was upon us. Elections were held annually in the 1950s, on the first Monday of December. Candidates signed up two weeks in advance. My mind was made up. I would step down from council and devote my energies entirely to the Leacock Home Committee. Perhaps Lou Ruby might be persuaded to become our renaissance prince. Nominations were filed on a Monday in late November; those nominated had twenty-four hours (to 8:00 p.m. the following day) to qualify as bona fide candidates or sign off. A ratepayers meeting at the Opera House followed the filing of nominations. These affairs were usually slanging matches, particularly when the mayoralty was up for grabs. Some ratepayers entered their names, just to grab a little platform time to chastise the current council. Immediately afterward, their civic duty done, they would tear up their nominations. As a rule, that still left a long list of genuine candidates. But not that particular night in 1956. I was reeve that year (Orillia's chief representative on Simcoe County Council) and was nominated for re-election to that office, as well as for deputy reeve and alderman. I told the ratepayers meeting that this was my swan song and that I intended to pursue the Leacock home purchase outside council.[3]

Withdrawing from the reeveship gave the office, by acclamation, to Jack McDonald, my detractor at the time of the Coronation gift proposal. Jack had expected a fight. The deputy reeveship went to Leacock supporter Bill Greer, again by acclamation. For the first time in living memory, at the end of the evening only seven names remained in the aldermanic contest, with six to be elected. Mine was one of the seven. If I went through with my swan song there would be no election in Orillia in December 1956! Worse, one of the six candidates who would win by acclamation was the town's leading eccentric. If elected, he would spread chaos at City Hall. On Tuesday morning I was called out several times from a county council session in Barrie to take urgent calls from my Orillia council colleagues. They told me that if I quit, I would be consigning them to certain hell for the next twelve months. By dinner time I knew what I had to do. I called my fellow councillors one by one. They wanted something from me, I wanted something from them. I asked each of them the following question: If I ran, campaigning on the single issue of the town's purchase of the Leacock home and got a high vote, would they consider that a mandate from taxpayers to proceed with the purchase of the property? All of them said yes. Just before eight o'clock that night, I signed my nomination papers. An aldermanic contest was assured.

For two weeks, I argued the merits of Orillia acquiring the Leacock home at ratepayers meetings in the south and west wards, emphasizing the bonus it would represent to Orillia's tourist economy. This time there was no back talk from my fellow councillors. On 3 December, election day, I placed second, a handful of votes behind newcomer Isabel Post. A week later, on Monday 10 December 1956, my colleagues kept their part of the bargain. A motion was approved, unanimously, authorizing the town to enter into negotiations for the purchase of the home of Stephen Leacock and an adjoining acre of land. That night the committee broke out the champagne. The next day a congratulatory letter arrived from an elated Hale. "Dear Pete," it began, "We have been through so much in these past few years, I feel I know you well enough to call you by your Christian name, and I would be honoured if you would do the same to me."[4]

Chapter 6

WAITING ON OTTAWA, 1957

On 28 January 1957 Orillia Town Council instructed its solicitor to draw up a by-law covering terms of a negotiated sale of the home to the town. Once purchased, the property was to be in the hands of the Orillia Parks Board until such time as a Leacock foundation could take responsibility. I told council that Lou Ruby intended to turn over the material contents of the home as a gift to the town and was planning a luxury subdivision for the remainder of the property. Now that Orillia had taken the critical first step, I was confident senior government would shower dollars upon us. Mayor Wilbur Cramp observed, "There may be some apathy on this project at the moment, but on the other hand we would be criticized if we lost this opportunity to get the Leacock home and library. In the long run (assuming senior governments contributed) it may not cost the town more than about ten thousand dollars."[1] On a Monday evening two months later, the by-law received its three readings without a dissenting vote. The following Friday Ruby came to town for the formal handover. He posed for a picture, accepting a gift copy of *Sunshine Sketches* from Mayor Cramp, moments after the Toronto publisher was handed a cheque for $25,000. In return he gave the mayor the property deed and a letter donating the contents of the home to the town. Now we owned it all – the home and all its treasures. It was a moment we had dreamed of, but reality soon caught up with us. What the town owned was a derelict summer mansion in desperate need of a new roof and front porch, a thousand windowpanes, and huge amounts of paint, stucco, putty and plaster. Lawns had to be cleared of jungle growth, and new

gardens set out. The Parks Board budgeted $2000 for the most urgent repairs. Alderman Bill Greer and I were both members of the Parks Board and were immediately constituted as a subcommittee to carry out repairs and start our planning for a museum. With the Parks Board's blessing, we set aside $250 to engage Ralph Curry for the summer of 1957.

Two thousand dollars was a pittance. It was time to search for major funding – the kind of money only senior governments could provide – to restore the home. Among C.H. Hale's admirers was Professor Fred Landon, head of the Department of History at the University of Western Ontario, then chair of the National Historic Sites and Monuments Board. Hale had kept him in the picture since the start-up of the Leacock Home Committee in October 1954. Landon's letters to Hale made it clear that he favoured public ownership and development of the home. At Hale's suggestion, Landon arranged an appointment for me in early January 1957 with A.J.H. Richardson, then chief of the National Historic Sites Division of the Department of Northern Affairs and National Resources. Richardson outlined several possibilities. If the board designated the home a national historic site we could apply for development grants. But we should be aware, he cautioned, that policy proposals were afloat that would restrict that designation to "homes of unusual architectural distinction or historic merit." It was up to the minister, Jean Lesage, to decide future policy. In extreme circumstances the board might be persuaded to buy the home outright and develop it as a federally operated museum. That possibility, however, was remote, since the home was already under the umbrella of a municipal government. Besides, the federal allotment for historic places was meagre. Frankly, he continued, the homes of humorists, no matter how celebrated, did not rank in national importance alongside Fort Royale, Nova Scotia or Fort Garry, Manitoba.[2]

I reported back to both the Parks Board and town council. Feelings were mixed. Mayor Cramp favoured a full federal takeover and was sure we could swing it. The Parks Board was pragmatic, believing that we should offer the National Historic Sites and Monuments Board some options – an outright takeover as Mayor Cramp proposed, or financial assistance to allow us to do the job ourselves. The sum of $15,000 was our objective. If we could get that much from Ottawa, we reasoned, a matching amount could be requested from the provincial government. To bolster our case, I flew to Ottawa on 10 March for a meeting arranged with Lesage. The mayor came along, as did Bill Moore, the town solicitor, the latter chiefly because he was a prominent Liberal and we were dealing with a Liberal government. Lesage was a large and hearty man who said he admired Leacock immensely and needed no convincing that our project was a worthy one. He would give the matter his earnest consideration. We came home in high spirits.

Our application was placed on the agenda of the June meeting of the National Historic Sites and Monuments Board. A formal presentation was needed and the Orillia Parks Board set to work on it. The mayor went to work, too. On 31 May, acting entirely on his own, he sent a letter to the Sites and Monuments Board proposing that the federal government take over the property, and compensate Orillia for the $25,000 already expended. The Parks Board had no choice but to back this approach. But since I would be delivering our presentation in Ottawa, I took it on myself to steer clear of an all-or-nothing proposition. Now began a comedy of errors. The meeting of the Historic Sites and Monuments Board was held on a Saturday morning in early June in a ministry office in Ottawa. I brought along property plans, photographs and a written presentation. The first page of the first draft (no other part of it survives) dwells on the character of Leacock:

> Stephen Leacock was more than a great humorist. He was a unique spokesman for a great era, a man whose literary scope was boundless, whose erudition, imagination, and keen understanding of human nature illuminated the sights, scenes and institutions around him during his lifetime and have made them unforgettable, for all of us. Leacock treated mankind with gentleness; his satire is infused with insight. Professor Leacock was the first to sketch the Canadian character of the twentieth century in a manner understandable to all other people.[3]

This should have impressed the board. The minutes of the meeting (which I did not see for thirty-four years) give a very different and bizarre account of my remarks. The most bizarre is this gem: "Alderman McGarvey, in reply to a question by Dr. Saga, answered that Professor Leacock was an American but his work was of great importance to Canada."[4] An American? What I said was that Leacock enjoyed an enormous following in the United States, even though he was a Canadian.

There is more. According to the minutes, I outlined the history of the town's acquisition of the home from Ruby, then continued with a description of the repairs and restoration work urgently required – "the installation of a new heating system, an exterior paint job, the cleaning and revarnishing of the floors, the re-shingling of the roof, and some repairs to the basement floor and in the billiard room. Additional requirements would be period furnishings, library shelving, and display cases. It was estimated the overall cost for restoration would be approximately $30,000, in addition to the $2000 already appropriated."[5] Later in the minutes:

Alderman McGarvey asked at this point that the home be considered of national importance because of the importance of Professor Leacock. He stated Town authorities, failing favourable consideration by the Board, would be prepared to proceed with the plan for a museum or Leacock shrine, housing in its upper stories a museum of local items considered to be of national importance, such as the heirlooms of pioneer families and the trophies of champion athletes. The alderman, in answering a question by Professor Landon stated that the Parks Board are prepared to assume responsibility for the future maintenance of the house and for the appointment of a curator to administer the building as a museum and Leacock Shrine ... Professor Landon explained to Alderman McGarvey that the policy concerning the restoration and preservation of old buildings had been before the Minister and the Board for review for some time. The Chairman stated further that the proposal would be given proper consideration and dealt with in accordance with the Minister's direction on policy.[6]

If that was supposed to mean "we're awaiting further word from Jean Lesage on this one," it was grossly misleading. Immediately after I left the room (as I learned thirty-four years later) a decision was made on The Old Brewery Bay. The minutes read:

Mr. Fiset remarked that the Leacock house itself does not fall within the description of what he regards as a building of national interest by reason of age or architectural design. The chairman stated he was inclined to agree with Mr. Fiset and considered the house to be an elaborate summer residence. It was therefore moved by Mr. Smith and seconded by Mr. Fiset that the name of Stephen Leacock be added to the list of eminent Canadians and that a secondary tablet be erected.[7]

That was strange. I had cast a broad net, pitching first for a federally owned and operated site, but if that wasn't in the cards, then for cash to help develop an Orillia-run museum. The minutes make no mention of this request, although I was quite specific about it in my presentation. We needed $30,000. I had hoped to find $15,000 of it in Ottawa and the balance at Queen's Park. Ignorance is indeed bliss. Unaware of the already decided outcome, I returned to Orillia buoyed by the reception of the board.

Less that two weeks later, on 21 June 1957, Canadian voters ended twenty-two years of Liberal rule, electing 112 Tories and only 105 Liberals. John Diefenbaker became prime minister and Orillia surgeon Philip B. (Doc) Rynard replaced Liberal Bill Robinson as the member for Simcoe East.

We wasted no time getting Doc Rynard into the picture. This affable Orillia surgeon had been reading Leacock since childhood and assured us that he was with us, heart and soul. Eager to help the cause, he intended to speak to the new minister of northern affairs, a Saskatchewan school principal named Alvin Hamilton, and urge him to give serious consideration to the Leacock home. Rynard also promised to search out the recommendations of the National Historic Sites and Monuments Board after the June meeting. Despite the doctor's valiant efforts, we heard nothing from Ottawa until 22 November, when I received an informal letter from Fred Landon with some startling revelations. According to the chairman of the Historic Sites and Monuments Board, Jean Lesage had written the board in advance of the June meeting rejecting the claims of both the Leacock home and the Brantford birthplace of poet Pauline Johnson as places of national importance! "I could not agree," Lesage stated, "that a building should be preserved because of the 'literary' or 'sentimental' values involved because this is not within the scope of the act I must administer."[8] Landon then explained that since a recommendation for aid was impossible, our application had been rejected and a motion passed to add the name of Stephen Leacock to the list of eminent Canadians. Leacock was to be honoured with the erection of a suitable tablet somewhere, sometime. The letter ended with a glimmer of hope. Lesage's note to the board was a statement of policy, which was not part of the statute governing the board. The new minister, Alvin Hamilton, might feel differently. Professor Landon urged us to pursue the matter with Hamilton.

It had taken seven months to learn, off the record, what the National Historic Sites and Monuments Board had decided. All now depended on Hamilton. Rynard inquired again. Again we were told to wait. The year 1957 ended with no word from Ottawa. By the second week of January 1958, Jim Lamb's patience had worn out. In a *Packet* editorial titled "PRESERVATION OF LEACOCK'S HOME DESERVES NATIONAL AID," Lamb joined the editor of *Saturday Night* in deploring Ottawa's refusal to offer even moral backing to Orillia's effort to preserve the home of "the foremost Canadian man of letters and one of the world's greatest humorists." The editorial talked of the Parks Board's hopes of persuading Hamilton to provide some kind of financial support. Even a token amount would suffice to attract other contributors. In the final paragraph Lamb went for the jugular:

But if the present government is so short-sighted and indifferent as to be unable to spare a few dollars to encourage this addition to the country's cultural heritage, then it must risk the displeasure of cultured people everywhere and of the thousands of Canadians who will be concerned at its inaction. Orillians, and indeed all Canadians will have an opportunity to register their protest at the next federal elections, which are expected this year.[9]

A few hours before the editorial appeared Lamb read it to me over the phone and informed me that he had dispatched a copy by special delivery to Alvin Hamilton's office in Ottawa.

Thirty-six hours later Doc Rynard was on the phone from Ottawa, pushing the panic button. He told me that he had just been raked over the coals by the minister over an editorial Rynard had not even seen! Hamilton wanted an immediate meeting with representatives of the Orillia Parks Board, and Rynard was to attend, too. The minister was not pleased, he warned me. Thursday 23 January was the date chosen. Deputy Reeve Bill Greer, my Leacock partner on council and Parks Board, joined me for the flight to Ottawa. We told the *Packet* we intended to press the minister for a grant – we hoped as high as $25,000.[10] It was a bold gesture. According to Rynard, there was no chance of mollifying the minister. On that fateful Thursday a number of Rynard's parliamentary colleagues assembled in his office to join us for the trip to the lion's den: Clayton Hodgson, parliamentary assistant to the minister of public works; John Hamilton, parliamentary assistant to the minister of citizenship and immigration; and George Doucette, a newly elected member of Parliament who had served for many years as Ontario's minister of highways. All these people were Leacock devotees, ready to back federal support of the project. When our deputation entered the office of the minister of northern affairs, we found him pacing up and down, a cold cigar in his mouth and a copy of the *Packet* in his hand. He did not waste time on niceties. He was not going to be intimidated by any small-town newspaper, he told us. We had known since last June that the National Historic Sites and Monuments Board could not do anything for us, so why this constant agitation? I told him that apart from the informal letter I had from Fred Landon in November, we had heard nothing from the Sites and Monuments Board. "That was impossible," the minister insisted. He instructed his secretary to get A.H.J. Richardson on the phone. When Richardson came on the line the minister asked him to pull the file on our application and read him the letter sent out after the June meeting. Richardson called back a few minutes later to say that there had been a slip-up. No letter had been sent. Somehow, we had fallen between the cracks. Richardson was sorry. The minister was even sorrier. He offered an apology and said that he felt he had to make amends in some way. No, he continued, he could not change the board's decision, but he did have some discretionary authority of his own and would use it to come up with a grant of some kind. The restoration could proceed now, he added, and the money would be soon available. Hamilton ended the meeting by asking that the Orillia public know of his decision.

In a front-page *Packet* story the following day, I noted that "everyone contacted, including the minister himself had been most interested and helpful and paid particular tribute to the efforts on behalf of the project of Dr. Rynard, member for the district."[11]

The story also said that the minister hoped to convene a meeting of the Historic Sites and Monuments Board at the Leacock home to see what assistance it could provide us. Where that came from is uncertain. It was not my understanding. As far as I knew, Hamilton intended to "end run" the board. And so it proved. On 26 March I had an excited phone-call from Rynard informing me that the minister was granting us $15,000 – not to restore the house, mind you, but to maintain an historic plaque to be erected sometime in the future on the Leacock verandah. Ingenious! But the announcement put me in a bind. Electors were going to the polls on 31 March. Rynard was the Progressive Conservative candidate in East Simcoe. The law forbade the media from publishing political news, in particular, news of grants and government largesse, for forty-eight hours before an election, excluding Sundays. The prohibition, therefore, was in place the day the doctor called me. I could not report the best news I had heard in a year without risking official protests from the Liberal and New Democratic Party camps. Rynard understood. He didn't need the boost anyway. On election day he easily trounced Liberal John MacIsaac and New Democrat Wilf Hoult in the second of six victories he would chalk up in more than twenty years in the federal arena.

On 1 April 1958 the countdown began at The Old Brewery Bay. Opening day was to be 5 July. By making our $15,000 do the work of more than three times that amount, and by recruiting a lot of volunteers, we felt we just might make the deadline.

Chapter Seven

A DREAM COMES TRUE, 1958

A season of miracles. In little more than ninety days during the spring of 1958, Stephen Leacock's home was brought back to life. The year before, a one-time grant of $5000 from the town and $2000 budgeted by the Parks Board made for a substantial start to the restoration. By mid-May 1957 we had finished the heavier and more necessary jobs. The front verandah had been rebuilt and repainted. New tar and sealing material had been applied to all the second-story porches and the top of the house. Several strips of cedar shingles had been torn off and replaced. All broken windows were replaced, and locks installed on all doors. The lawn had had its initial cutting. Dampness had caused the billiard room floor to heave in a dozen places. The doors and windows were opened and a fire lit, so that the floor was sinking back to its normal level. The house had been measured out so that a complete lay-out could be prepared, showing the original uses of each room. Electricians had checked the entire house to see what would be required, and plumbers had reviewed the water situation.[1]

A month later Ralph Curry, his wife and two young daughters were in full-time residence at The Old Brewery Bay, and Curry was doing the circuit of Orillia service clubs to report on the progress of the restoration and sign up volunteers to help with the scrub-down and painting of the home. The membership of the Parks Board subcommittee dealing with the house expanded. Joining Bill Greer and myself were Maude Ardagh and Marjorie Tudhope. The ladies knew every nook and cranny of his home – where certain furniture had been placed, what lamps went where, how each room was decorated. Some armchairs, wicker furniture and lamps, along with a few bedsteads, wooden chairs and tables, had survived the years of abandonment All the furniture was restored and used in the home. Charlie Greenwood had a new project now. His plans for a gorgeous lawn and new flower-beds were on paper by March 1957. Since the restoration was under the auspices of the Orillia Parks Board, sod, seedlings, soil and labour were available on request. Charlie's vision, his uncanny green thumb and his unstinting, unpaid labour over many weeks worked wonders. Before the summer of 1957 ended, flowers bloomed everywhere and the lawn was a rich green. According to Maude Ardagh and others, Stephen Leacock's lakefront looked just the way it had two decades before. Cliff Peters, the *Packet*'s city editor, was another busy committee member, creating a "before and after" pictorial record of the restoration.

John Drainie came up with a bold scheme that summer – a Leacock Memorial Theatre in Orillia to stage adaptations of the works of Leacock and other Canadian humorists. Drainie would be artistic director, not to mention chief Leacock adapter and the portrayer of the man himself. The theatre would attract visitors to the home, and vice-versa. An application to the Canada Council for a founding grant for the theatre, however, was turned down. The Canada Council looked with uncertainty on Canadian humour. Earlier it had declined an invitation from the Leacock Associates to take over the judging of entries for the Stephen Leacock Medal for Humour (and to provide a cash award to the winner), making it clear in its response that the council did not rank the production of humour in the same creative category as poetry or prose. What might Leacock have made of the Canada Council?

Drainie kept the theatre proposal alive for several years, but with virtually no interest shown by funding agencies or foundations, finally abandoned it. Instead he took his one-man Leacock show on the road, performing across Canada and Britain.

Our immediate financial crisis ended on 27 March 1958. Within days of Hamilton's announcement the Orillia Parks Board met to discuss the expenditure of the $15,000 grant and the long-term administration of the property. The 1957 development plan was dusted off and adopted. It called for permanent, glassed-in shelves for a library, to be installed in what had been the lakeside ground-floor bedroom of Leacock's day. Four custom-built, lighted showcases would be placed here, making it the principal display area. The rear bedroom, Leacock's own, would be Curry's study and the home's archive centre. The 1929 gas range in the kitchen was still in place. We converted it to electricity and it is still in use. We tracked down a 1920s vintage ice box and installed it in the kitchen. Maude Ardagh donated a walnut dining room set – a handsome sideboard, table and chairs – observing that they were fancier than anything seen in Leacock's time. We bought period furniture for the living room to complement the wicker chairs and sofas discovered in the basement the previous year. We budgeted for a long list of electrical and plumbing jobs to assure that our museum passed all safety regulations. Ralph Curry's salary for the upcoming summer was set at $1000. And there was a small budget for a handyman and three guides, who would be trained in June and early July. To administer the property we asked for our own board. The Orillia Town Council and Orillia Parks Board quickly granted the request. On 28 May 1958 the Stephen Leacock Memorial Home Board came into being, consisting of Grace Crooks (as secretary), Maude Ardagh, Charlie Greenwood, James B. Lamb, Kenneth C. Bath (general manager of the Orillia Chamber of Commerce), Mrs. Jack Oatway (a representative of the Women's Institute) and town council appointee Alderman George A.N. McLean. Ralph Curry was an ex-officio member, and I was chairman. Lamb, Ardagh, Greenwood, Oatway and I were holdovers from the old Leacock Home Committee, which had been dissolved in March 1957.

The opening day of the Stephen Leacock Memorial Home – 5 July – came little more than a month after the formation of the board. Invitations to the event were mailed to a long list of notables, beginning with Governor General Vincent Massey. In the weeks running up to our grand opening, scaffolding framed large areas of the house as painters from the Orillia firm of McPhee Paint and Wallpaper applied a fresh coat of white with green trim. Inside, floors were scrubbed, scraped and sanded, panelling polished and furniture moved in. The library showed the handicraft of Willie Goodall, Willie Hislop and Bill Budchuck. Budchuck built the library display cases, while the two Willies, Scottish-born partners in a firm that specialized in quality housing, constructed the glass-enclosed bookshelves on four walls of the room, replacing "shelves" Leacock had built himself – a series of uprights with rough boards placed between and nailed into place. Drapery for the home came from Anderson Furniture; plumbing was restored by Jack Oatway and Sons. The craftsmen and suppliers were all enthusiastic about the project and were willing to wait for their money. The federal grant arrived in installments; months would pass before the last of our contractors was paid.

Opening day was an unabashed triumph. Governor General Massey did not attend, nor did young Stevie, but almost everyone else on our mailing list did. Alvin Hamilton was driven from Ottawa by Doc Rynard. (Thirty-five years later, Gordon Aiken, the former member of Parliament for Muskoka, told me that he accompanied the minister from the capital that morning and the memory of the trip still haunted him. Rynard, a driver of legendary speed and rashness, was their chauffeur. Hamilton and Aiken were sure they would never reach Orillia alive!) Leslie Frost was front and centre, too, along with Bill Cranston. Two days before the opening, Ottawa rushed us a set of directional signs. Cranston offered to erect them even though they would carry a federal rather than a provincial coat-of-arms. Here was the first provincial contribution to the Leacock cause in four years, and we were led to hope that the door to Queen's Park was now open. Frost's warm praise for Leacock and Orillia at a noon luncheon and later at the two o'clock opening ceremony bolstered that hope.

At both the luncheon and opening, I took care to see that everybody was thanked – my fellow Orillians, the politicians, the volunteers, the media, the literary community – singling out William Arthur Deacon, Louis Blake Duff, Gladstone Murray and B.K. Sandwell, all friends and professional associates of the great humorist. From the luncheon at the Stephen Leacock Pavilion in Orillia's Couchiching Beach Park, the official party moved in antique autos to The Old Brewery Bay where two hundred townspeople were waiting along with a score of reporters. The brave sounds of the Orillia Kiltie and Orillia Silver bands echoed over the bay. On the verandah, after the playing of "O Canada," Stephen Leacock was lauded by one speaker after another – Mayor Art Truman, Lloyd Letherby, MPP for Simcoe East, Frost, Simcoe County Warden Art Evans, C.H. Hale, Ralph Curry, Doc Rynard, and Alvin Hamilton, in that order. It was grand and serious stuff, full of the hyperbole Orillians of a generation ago loved to hear in their public ceremonies.[2]

Rynard gave the day a Leacock touch it lacked, though he did so in all innocence. Wessely Hicks reported the opening in the Toronto *Telegram* as follows:

> It was a solemn occasion and yet in some ways a gay occasion. The bands were playing on the lawn. The old house was primped up in a new coat of white paint and looked rather like a girl in a white crinoline at a garden party. Boats danced and cavorted out on the lake. The breezes whispered through the great old trees. The people who had gathered on the lawn were in saucy summer clothes. And throughout the whole ceremony a black bird whipped in and out from under the eaves of the old house.
>
> There were speeches on Saturday. A solemn occasion is always made more solemn by pouring speeches over it.
>
> So you stood there waiting for someone to say that Mariposa was officially incorporated and could be marked on all up-to-date maps. But no one did. After a while you watched the black bird popping in and out from under the

eaves. You nearly missed Dr. P.B. Rynard, the member of Parliament for Simcoe East.

Dr. Rynard strayed a mite in his speech. He wandered by way of the Trent Canal and the Champlain monument. He came in over Lake Couchiching, which, he said, lapped the very shore of the property where the house stands. "Lake Couchiching," he said, "the very same waters that Champlain trod."

You knew then that no one had to say that Mariposa was real.

It is.[3]

When the speeches ended, we moved to the front door. Handed a pair of shears to cut a ribbon and a golden key to open the door, Hamilton turned to Hale and asked him to join him. It was a generous gesture. At five minutes to four on Saturday afternoon, 5 July 1958, the front door swung open at The Old Brewery Bay and the world was invited in.

Hicks was right. Mariposa had come to life again in the summer of 1958. No sooner were opening ceremonies completed, and a plaque unveiled in the library acknowledging Lou Ruby's extraordinary gift, than visitors began to arrive. For many of them the home was a magnificent discovery. In the library showcases were placed Leacock's earliest letters. They were arranged alongside photographs of him as a child and head boy at Upper Canada College and more photographs from sunny days in turn-of-the-century Orillia as a member of the local cricket club. There were handwritten letters and manuscripts along with correspondence from famous people, including Prime Minister R.B. Bennett and F. Scott Fitzgerald, and books with special significance in Leacock's life – a first edition of *Literary Lapses* (1910), Leacock's first published volume of humour, and a copy of *Canada, The Foundation of Its Future,* which was published privately by the Seagram Corporation during the Second World War. There was also the folder titled "Letters From Damn Fools," which I had found in 1955. And Leacock's own fishing pole. Hundreds of books, many of them personally enscribed to Leacock, filled the glassed-in shelves. As visitors toured each room of the house, they came to appreciate the many intricacies of Leacock's life. The guides explained how, when and why he chose this particular spot on Lake Couchiching for his home and why the home's architectural features include both English country home panelling and Spanish stucco. The guides also explained when and where he wrote in the home – in his bedroom, in the study nearby, on sunny but chilly days in the sun porch at the rear, and in the earliest morns of summer on the second floor of the boathouse. With only the murmur of birds and the gentle splash of early waking bass in the bay to disturb him, he was in his element in the boathouse. Later, over breakfast, he would often read what he had written to his guests. His brother George told me in 1947 that sometimes the piece would be so funny that Stephen would literally choke on his own laughter and find it impossible to continue. After breakfast, time was allotted for gardening, construction projects, trips to town and, above all, fishing, sailing and convivial entertaining.

Curry trained the guides well. In little more than two weeks before our doors opened, they were steeped in the anecdotal lore that surrounded Leacock's summer haven. Visitors would be shown what at first glance looked like a hidden compartment in a bookshelf wall of the professor's study. "Did Leacock hide his whisky here, as rumour had it?" they would ask. "No – Leacock never hid a bottle of whisky in his life!" they would answer. By sliding open the door of this "secret compartment," Leacock could peek through a telephone closet into the dining and living rooms to check on his guests.

Visitors saw the Leacock study adjoining the new library, the dining room, living room and kitchen, but nothing more, at least in the summer of 1958. The upper floor and the basement were off limits. The Currys lived upstairs and the billiard room, like the sun porch, was still in ruins.

That summer the media came and were impressed; the restored Leacock home was a major story across Canada. And celebrities arrived. Few days passed without some notable politician, author or actor turning up to pay homage to Leacock. Among the first guests were Chief Justice and Mrs. Patrick Kerwin. The country's foremost jurist was a rotund, soft-voiced gentleman, reserved in manner but armed with a dry, sly sense of humour that owed everything to the influence of Stephen Leacock. Few people knew it, but the chief justice escaped Ottawa for Lake Simcoe every summer. He and his wife were guests of Jack and Grace Baker of Cedarhurst Beach, near Beaverton. The Kerwins made an informal visit to The Old Brewery Bay in the summer of 1956 and were so impressed that they called the next summer as well, while preliminary restoration work was under way. They came back every year for the next decade.

The day after Labour Day I took a phone call from a Muskoka resort. It was Thomas B. Costain. The Brantford-born editor and novelist was winding up a holiday and leaving for New York the next day, but wanted to see The Old Brewery Bay on his way through Orillia. Costain had been a close friend and professional associate of the humorist since the early years of the century. Leacock had entertained him many times in both Montreal and Orillia. Costain was a large, white-thatched man in his seventies. He spoke sparingly and quietly but with passion. For an hour we toured a home he had known well in bygone days. Again and again he was emotionally stirred, his recollection triggered by a picture or a piece of furniture. Even the billiard room, with its heaved floors and flaking paint and collapsed table, held precious memories. Later, sitting on the front porch, we talked for forty minutes and I taped the conversation. He remembered congenial company, parties in the parlour and picnic spreads in warm weather on the lawn. He recalled Leacock as one of nature's true works-of-art, blessed with both literary genius and a common touch. And he remembered the last time he had seen him alive. Fifteen years earlier Costain had parked his car in almost exactly the spot it now occupied and was walking up the front path when Leacock came bursting from the house, waving a piece of paper and roaring with laughter. "Costain," he bellowed, "you've got to see this. It's a letter from a professor in Chicago who's doing an anthology on absent-minded professors. And the damn fool forgot to sign his name!"

At the end of our talk Costain lavished praise on the efforts to preserve and restore Leacock's summer estate. All was right, he said. The house looked comfortable and lived-in, just as Leacock had known it in the thirties. Leacock had been, Costain reflected, no more the slave of furnishing fashions than he had been of literary fads. He would no doubt approve the restoration. Thomas Costain's visit capped a summer of dazzling days at The Old Brewery Bay. It also represented a vote of approval from one of Leacock's professional peers for what was happening in Orillia.

Chapter Eight

THE DREAM EXPANDS, 1959–1960

More than five thousand people paid fifty cents each to make the pilgrimage journey to The Old Brewery Bay between 5 July and 3 September 1958. Admissions and postcard sales easily recovered our operating costs. Town of Orillia by-law 3627, passed on 29 May 1958, directed the newly appointed board to use admissions, grants-in-aid, sale of souvenirs and other such methods to finance ongoing operations. If there was a deficit at the end of the year the Leacock Home Board could requisition town council to cover it. Surpluses were to be used "to keep alive and spread interest in Stephen Leacock and his works."[1]

From the beginning, The Old Brewery Bay was cursed by its uniqueness. Government bureaucrats hate something that does not fit, that cannot be pigeonholed, or that threatens to establish a precedent. Our project refused to fit into any pigeonholes. No other municipality in Canada owned and operated a literary museum of international standing. Everything that happened at the Leacock home after 1958 established precedents and often stirred up controversy.

The $15,000 grant from Ottawa was a one-time donation. From 1959 on, we received a $1000 annual museum support grant from the Ontario government. That same year Orillia Town Council pledged an annual grant of $600 a year towards our operating budget. In the search for outside financial help, from 1958 to 1960 Ralph Curry sent out appeals to foundations on both sides of the border. They were asked to consider taking on individual projects at the home, of which there was a plentiful supply. We came up empty-handed but kept trying. One strong possibility was the Bronfman Foundation or one of the breweries or distilleries then distributing thousands of dollars annually for cultural causes. Why not make a pitch to one of them on behalf of The Old Brewery Bay? It would have solved a lot of problems, but it would also have mortified C.H. Hale, who had spent a lifetime fighting "the liquour interests." Out of respect for him, the idea was dropped.

The 1958 restoration exhausted the federal government's $15,000 grant as well as $7000 put up earlier by the town and the Parks Board. There was still much to do, as a 1959 wish list shows, with estimated costs attached:

1. Two rooms on first floor for restoration and conversion to staff lounge (the old servants quarters) $1000.
2. Study Centre on second floor, shelving, showcases, file cabinets and furniture $2500.
3. 'Mariposa' Room on second floor, to contains items relative to SUNSHINE SKETCHES – Orillia mementos of period covered in book $1000.
4. Billiard Room; new floor, repainted walls, new fixtures $1000.
5. Billiard Room: re-building billiard table (Brunswick-Balke-Collender) $400.
6. Heating system: double or single heating unit with gas-burners, new ductwork, insulation, etc. $6500.
7. Property purchase: Cost $4500 per lot for Lots 23, 24, 25 and adjacent lots for landscaping.
8. Acquisition of gatehouse lodge and adjacent property for eventual conversion to display space – $10,000.
9. Construction of wharf in Old Brewery Bay for access to property by water. Dredging? Construction $1000.
10. Acquisition of further original furniture (through S. Leacock Jr) $1000.
11. Floors – further work $1500.[2]

One major project not on the list was the reconstruction of the sun porch. To the rescue came Wessely Hicks. A few weeks after the close of our first season I met Hicks in his office at the Toronto *Telegram* to discuss the momentum that had been created and what remained to be done. He felt that we needed input from a couple of kindred souls at the newspaper, Laurie McKechnie and Bas Mason. McKechnie was the *Telegram*'s old-timer. A veteran of the journalistic wars against the *Toronto Star*, he was now ensconced as editorial assistant to owner-publisher John Bassett. More importantly, he was the paper's literary editor. Bas Mason was the paper's promotions director. We walked from Wess's cubbyhole to the unadorned office where Laurie McKechnie watched over the fortunes of a paper he had served as reporter and editor for a quarter-century. Doors at the *Telegram* were never closed and rank rarely pulled. McKechnie was the most improbable of editorial managers. Far from the stereotypical hard-bitten and terrible-tempered newsroom boss, he radiated a fatherly and kindly spirit, chuckled easily and often, and showed within minutes not only a broad appreciation of Leacock but a willingness to put the paper behind any scheme to help the Leacock home! The three of us moved down the hall and barged into Bas Mason's office. Mason, like McKechnie, set aside current business and put his mind to the challenge at hand. In ten minutes the plan was formed. Early in 1959 the *Telegram* would sponsor a "Meet the Authors" Dinner at the Royal York Hotel. One hundred published Canadian writers would be guests-of-honour, each hosting a table of paying guests. We would ask the support of the Canadian Authors Association and would enlist the CBC's Mavor Moore, Don Harron and Norman Campbell, who were responsible for *Sunshine Town,* a popular musical based on *Sunshine Sketches of a Little Town.* John Drainie would be signed up and a host of other entertainers engaged. Proceeds from the dinner would be used to rebuild the sun porch at The Old Brewery Bay.

We met several more times at the *Telegram* office as autumn turned to winter. McKechnie took charge. He recruited Jack McClelland, president of McClelland and Stewart and Leacock's publisher. McClelland was the only person in Toronto who could match Bas Mason in promotional zeal. The publisher in turn pulled in the Canadian Authors Association, the Canadian Library Week Council (the dinner was to be staged Thursday 16 April, during Canadian Library Week) and his fellow publishers. Teaser stories began to appear in the *Telegram* in early January 1959. By early March, 800 tickets for the dinner were on sale, at ten dollars per seat. By 10 April the dinner was sold out.

The night was dazzling. Assembled in the concert hall of the Royal York Hotel were sixty published writers, almost every Canadian author then appearing in print, among them Ralph Allen, Will E. Bird, Morley Callaghan, Gregory Clark, Mazo de la Roche, Mary Quayle Innis, W.G. Hardy, Leslie Ruth Howard, William Kilbourn, Roger Lemelin, Ned Pratt and Harry Symons. The dress was formal but not the program. There were no speeches, except for official greetings from the provincial attorney-general and brief expressions of gratitude from Ralph Curry and myself. Entertainment made the evening. In addition to the selections from *Sunshine Town,* performed by a CBC chorus, Mariposa was evoked through "Old

Brewery Bay," a song written for the occasion, with music by Norman Campbell and lyrics by Elaine Campbell. John Drainie appeared as Stephen Leacock. The Don Wright Singers and a CBC dance troupe performed. Max "Rawhide" Ferguson presented "Fighting Words," a parody of the popular CBC panel show. Eric Christmas, Elizabeth Cole, Tony Van Bridge and Mary Savage presented "The Reading Public," a dramatization of the Leacock essay.

The true costs of the evening remained a mystery. Publishers shelled out for the authors' dinner tickets and travel expenses. Entertainment was paid for by corporate sponsors, whose arms had been twisted by Bas Mason. The dinner also produced a surprise. When Kenneth Noxon read about it in the newspaper, he searched his company's archives and retrieved the original plans of the Leacock home. He handed them over to Ralph Curry in mid-1959. The blueprints made possible a detailed restoration of the original sun porch. And the $6000 generated by the "Meet the Authors" Dinner assured a quality job.

The finishing touches on the sun porch owed everything to the Karsh portraits of 1941. Ralph Curry pored over the pictures to learn exactly where chairs, tables and other furniture had been placed twenty years earlier. In the centre of a rack on the east wall was a grandfather clock, the works removed and the face replaced with an eight-day alarm clock – a Leacock joke of many years before. Curry located this altered antique in the basement of the caretaker's lodge, cleaned it up and positioned it exactly where it had been in 1941. The rack, though, had to be rebuilt. On it we hung a battered fedora, similar to the one that appears in the original photographs, along with a golf club, an antique tennis racquet and other paraphernalia. The six-sided book rack beside Leacock's work table was found intact, and restored to its original spot after a paint job, Above it we hung a pail, just as shown in the 1941 portrait.

The official opening of the sun porch was scheduled for Saturday 11 June 1960 as part of the Leacock Medal Dinner weekend. Once more, in the unfolding history of the restored home, irony enters the story. Pierre Berton won the 1960 Medal for Humour and was the centre of attention that Saturday in Orillia. The sun porch reopening was dramatic. A makeshift curtain covered the windows. Drainie, as Stephen Leacock, was seated at Leacock's work table at the east end of the porch, in precisely the same pose the humorist had struck for Yousuf Karsh in one of his 1941 portraits. Each person in the crowd outside was given a copy of the Karsh picture. A curtain was strung the entire length of the porch. When the curtain was dropped the effect was electrifying. Drainie, as Leacock, rose from the table and walked to the doorway, to read his "summer guests" a piece he had just written – about summer guests. It was a brilliant performance but it lost out, in news coverage, to Berton's appearance that night at Fern Cottage Resort before the largest crowd ever assembled for a Leacock Medal Dinner. The room rocked with laughter as he read selections from his prize-winning *Just Add Water and Stir*. Hicks, Mason and McKechnie, the *Telegram*'s incomparable trio, calmly accepted Berton's day of honour. To show that they were good sports they hosted a pre-dinner reception at the Orillia House for the man who was to rob them, single-handedly, of hundreds of readers over the years and who had just deprived them of their moment in the sun. Berton appreciated the gesture. Later that night he praised the *Telegram* for the success of its imaginative project and noted that in some things – such as supporting the Leacock legacy – there should be no rivalries.

To their dying days, Hicks, Mason and McKechnie remained loyal to The Old Brewery Bay. Stories about the Leacock home were a feature of Laurie's Saturday feature "Browsing" until his retirement in the late 1960s. Hicks's contributions are not forgotten. In 1959 he was chosen by the Leacock Associates as the first "Mayor of Mariposa," responsible for a tongue-in-cheek "state of the town" report at each Leacock dinner. He held the post for five years and was succeeded by Harry J. Boyle.

Bas Mason remains an unheralded hero of this story. There was his off-stage but critical role in the "Meet the Authors" Dinner in 1959 and far greater deeds afterwards. In 1969 Mason took a leading role in promoting the centennial of Leacock's birth. A national committee he helped organize in Toronto persuaded the federal government to issue a commemorative stamp. Thirty-four million were printed. Also at the committee's urging, Ottawa named a mountain for our greatest humorist. Mount Stephen Leacock is in the Elias range, between the Yukon and the Northwest Territories. The Ontario government was asked to name an Orillia area provincial park after Leacock and designate a new Toronto to Lake Simcoe highway "The Leacock Road." Neither proposal won approval. Elsewhere across the land, but in Montreal, Toronto and Orillia especially, the committee promoted commemorative dinners, literary seminars and special library programs to remind Canadians what they owed to Leacock. The Leacock story was told and retold in newspapers and magazines and through a host of television and radio specials. Behind most of these schemes Mason's promotional skill was discernible and as usual he shunned the spotlight. His name appeared on no letterheads. He hated even to have his picture taken. A candid shot at the "Meet the Authors" dinner is one of the few photos of this remarkable Canadian to be found in the public record.

In the mid-1960s Bas and his wife Jean had moved to Midland, where he served as development officer at Ste Marie-Among-the-Hurons, then under construction on the banks of the Wye River. With his usual enthusiasm he urged educators across the province to use the site as a living classroom. Leacock and The Old Brewery Bay were not forgotten. His proximity to Orillia allowed Mason to stay active in a cause that had grown dear to him. In 1966 he used his skills to persuade the Montreal Standard Publishing Company to purchase the handwritten manuscript of *Sunshine Sketches of a Little Town* from Barbara Nimmo. Ralph Curry accepted it on behalf of the home in a ceremony attended by Nimmo on 26 August 1966. Although Mason worked on behalf of the Leacock cause in Orillia in his own time, his Midland employers frowned on his activities and there was a parting of the ways. Mason was not deterred. He went on promoting Leacock and Mariposa until his death in 1988 in Powassan, Ontario, a year before Wessely Hicks died.

What about Pierre Berton, the 1960 medal winner who had inadvertently played the role of spoiler? His loyalty to Leacock and Orillia has also been constant through the years. And he always enters into the spirit of things. In June 1970, Berton's friend Farley Mowat received the Leacock medal. Berton, Mowat and Jack McClelland began their celebration early that afternoon beside Lake Couchiching. Mowat had come to Orillia proudly sporting his clan's tartan. There was much friendly banter between the dais and Berton's table as dinner proceeded. Just as the evening's speeches were getting under way, Berton demanded, in a loud voice, to know if Mowat was wearing his kilt properly. "I am, me son," Mowat shot back, leaping to his feet, turning his back to the audience and lifting his kilt. There was nothing underneath! Pandemonium ensued. People either gasped in horror or laughed hysterically. It was a moment like no other in the long, uninhibited history of Leacock feasts. Many years passed before McClelland or Berton felt it safe to return to Orillia. McClelland came back in June 1978 for a dinner honouring Ernest Buckler, author of *Whirligig*, which was published by McClelland and Stewart. On that occasion McClelland delivered an abject apology for his behaviour of a decade before, a lapse in good taste he attributed to too much Scotch and the bad influence of writers. As he spoke, with TV cameras whirring, he removed first his suit coat, then his shirt, to reveal a T-shirt bearing the words "Great In Bed – Call 211-4123!" Pierre Berton turned up, in 1985, to help honour his friend Ted Allan, author of the award-winner *Love Is a Long Shot*. Five years later he served as master of ceremonies when another old friend, W.O. Mitchell, was awarded his second Leacock medal. The occasion also marked the thirtieth anniversary of Berton's own win. The evening went without a hitch. Berton and Mitchell were in their element. Adjournment had been declared but Mitchell had one postscript to add – clarifying an earlier comment. His riposte was a gem, but it is remembered chiefly for the precedent it set. After forty-four years the "F" word had been uttered at a Leacock dinner!

During my Toronto years, I interviewed Farley Mowat many times and always coaxed him to return to Orillia for a Leacock festivity. He always refused. "It's too soon," he would say.

Chapter Nine

AFTERMATH

My story ends in 1960. The Old Brewery Bay's first three seasons were an enormous success. An important new cultural resource had been created. Scholars and devoted Leacock fans the world over were grateful. The sun porch had been restored, completing the original structure. And we had come to an understanding with town council on the future of The Old Brewery Bay. There was no longer talk of a Leacock foundation, or a federal buy-out of the property. Instead, council approved a long-term plan for capital projects, and agreed to pay off a $3500 deficit. By doing so, Orillia's municipal leaders served notice that they considered Stephen Leacock's estate and Mariposa lore the town's inheritance. Clearly, Orillia was benefiting from the media hype and increased tourism. There were still doubters and nay-sayers, and conflicts over funding and jurisdictions would go on (as Jay Cody's closing chapter records), but on the whole, Orillians were proud now to call themselves Mariposans.

If there was a defining moment in the process, it came on 4 July 1959, the day Queen Elizabeth and Prince Philip came to town and received as Orillia's official gift *Sunshine Sketches of a Little Town*. It was the same book the town fathers had voted not to forward as a Coronation gift six years earlier! The leather-bound, gold-embossed volume was prepared under the personal direction of Jack McClelland. In an appendix C.H. Hale wrote descriptive texts for a series of Orillia landmarks. The book was not stashed away by some palace flunky, as Alderman Jack McDonald once had predicted. Quite the opposite. The Queen's cross-country tour was interrupted for two days in Yellowknife for medical reasons. She picked up the book, read it from cover to cover and felt much better. The *Telegram* stumbled on the story and ran it as a Saturday feature, under Laurie McKechnie's byline. The Queen's indisposition proved to be a pregnancy. Prince Andrew, considered the wittiest of the royal offspring, was born six months later. Is it possible he owes his cheery nature to his mother's exposure to the immortal characters of Mariposa in the summer of 1959? McKechnie's article urges everyone to try Leacock's tonic

> for a good many of the rheums, tremors, flatulence and vapors suffered by the world today. The treatment, by the way, is considerably more efficacious if it is accompanied by a trip to the Leacock house at Old Brewery Bay. There the atmosphere plus the view over the lake, which Leacock once recommended to the Queen Mother, is guaranteed to restore perspective and bring relief from Trackus Rodentis (a medical term for Rat Race). Having exposed myself to the Old Brewery Bay elixir earlier this week, we are in a position to report Dr. Leacock's remedy is not exclusively effective for Queens. It is equally beneficial for ordinary folk, Angry Young Men or even Chicago-style novelists. A reading of Leacock plus an infusion of Old Brewery Bay atmosphere should, in fact, make the world appear a pleasant place in which to live.[1]

What visitors find at The Old Brewery Bay today is an elaborate summer home much as Stephen Leacock knew it. Since the rebuilding of the sun porch in 1960, the verandah has been rebuilt twice, the roof reshingled three times, and plumbing, heating and wiring updated. However, virtually no structural changes have been made to the 1928 design. What has changed are the uses and functions and furnishing of some rooms. Upstairs, for example, the east-end bedroom once considered the domain of René du Roure is used to display lecture posters from Leacock's 1921 tour of Britain, as well as mementos of Leacock broadcasts and posters from original melodramas staged right here in the home. In the first bedroom west of the hallway is an example of the "iron hospital beds" Elizabeth Kimball remembers. The chest near the bed was brought to Canada in 1876 by Agnes Leacock. Rumour has it that a ghost inhabits this room from time to time, but whose ghost is uncertain. The larger bedroom on the west side is now the Mariposa Room, housing an impressive pictorial display of Orillia in the first decade of the twentieth century, the time of *Sunshine Sketches*. Downstairs, the dining room, living room, kitchen, hallway, sun porch and study look as they did six decades earlier. In the living room, visitors see Leacock's own leather recliner in front of a poster advertising an Old Brewery Players presentation. From this recliner he could watch his servants through the mirror in the dining room. The servants' quarters, minus the dividing walls, is a museum office. Leacock's bedroom in the southeast corner of the house was used for archives storage until the opening of Swanmore Hall in 1994. The glassed-in bookshelves constructed in 1958 remain unchanged. The shelves accommodate 5000 books. An anteroom between the verandah and the library is a Leacock picture gallery. Here Yousef Karsh's 1941 portraits are on display and visitors can listen to a tape of the famed photographer talking about his visit to The Old Brewery Bay. In the basement, the billiard room is open again, thanks to the generosity of the Brunswick company. My brother George has been a life-long employee of Brunswick International (Canada) Ltd. and a Leacock enthusiast. He inspected the original table in 1966 and concluded that it was beyond repair. He then persuaded his company to install, at no charge, a comparable table, complete with matching equipment. The vintage six-by-twelve-foot English billiards table assembled in 1967 is worth several thousand dollars.

Local enthusiasm for one of Canada's most memorable writers and beloved characters grew impressively in the years after Orillia finally asserted its Mariposa heritage and opened the Leacock Museum. The Leacock Medal for Humour Dinners have lured the cream of Canada's literary life to Orillia year after year. The competition for the coveted medal attracts the nation's wittiest writers. In 1966 Manulife Insurance presented the winner with a $500 cheque. Later, the cash award came from the Hudson's Bay Company. From 1984 to 1994, Wiser Distillery offered a $3500 cash award. In 1994, Manulife Bank of Canada took over as corporate sponsor, providing a $5000 cheque to the winner. (See Appendix.) The *Newspacket*, launched in the spring of 1970 by John and Peggy Dyment and published several times a year, carries stories of the Leacock Associates, the Leacock Museum and Leacock literary developments (new biographies, etc.) to thousands of devotees across the world.

Other Leacock/Mariposa spinoffs include the Mariposa Folk Festival, launched in Orillia in 1961 by ·Dr. Casey and Ruth Jones; the Leacock Festival of Humour in the early 1970s, showcasing Canada's finest comedic talent on the Opera House stage (but strangely, offering little of Leacock's own humour); and the Leacock Heritage Festival, upgraded by Doug Little of the Downtown Management Board from a sidewalk sale promotion in the late 1980s to a full-blown award-winning ten-day program in the 1990s that pays more than lip service to the beloved humorist. Orillians are encouraged to dress in Edwardian fashions and promenade up and down the main street. At The Old Brewery Bay, crowds gather to hear the words of Stephen

Leacock and the works of Leacock medal winners, read by the winners themselves. Street-dances and Leacock shows at the Opera House are part of the annual program. *The Island Princess* loads up daily at the foot of Mississaga Street and carries sightseers past Leacock's Old Brewery Bay every summer. It sometimes stops at a new dock a hundred yards from the front door.

And what of the characters who played principal roles in this story?

RALPH CURRY's biography, *Stephen Leacock: Humorist and Humanist,* appeared in September 1959 and was hailed by William Arthur Deacon as the "definitive life of Leacock."[2] Year after year, for pathetically little pay and no long-term benefits, Curry journeyed from Georgetown, Kentucky, to Orillia, to continue his Leacock quest. He sorted, identified, and preserved thousands of articles, letters, sketches, business and legal correspondence, diaries, photographs and other memorabilia. He oversaw the guides and maintenance staff, worked with the board on operational and promotional strategies, made speeches and entertained the media. His courtly manners, easy laugh and Kentucky drawl endeared him to every audience. A surge of Canadian nationalism in the 1970s saw a new perspective emerge about the role of so-called "foreign" experts in our culture. Ralph was caught in the cross-fire and retired in 1977, to be succeeded by Jay Cody. On 1 December 1993 Jay Day was celebrated at the home to mark Jay's retirement and the start of a new era. His successor, Daphne Mainprize, like her predecessors, has brought to the curator's role great personal charm, impressive administrative skills and a deep appreciation of Leacock's abiding genius.

LESLIE FROST continued as Ontario's premier till November 1961, leading Ontario's Progressive Conservatives to victory in three successive elections. He retired to Lindsay, made frequent visits back to Orillia, and died on 4 May 1973.

CHARLES HAROLD HALE lived until 10 June 1963, agitating to the end for a greater Orillia. After 1954, we worked together twice more. I joined him in a successful campaign to rename the old Orillia Post Office as "The Sir Samuel Steele Building" to honour an Orillia-born hero of the Northwest Mounted Police. The second campaign, in 1962, didn't work out. It would have seen the Hale home, at 93 Mary Street, turned into a municipal museum upon his death. He deeded the residence and his vast collection of historical material to the town. But town council rejected the proposal. They already were supporting one museum which was running a deficit. When Hale died at the age of eighty-nine, his home was sold and proceeds donated to the Orillia Soldiers Memorial Hospital. But the Hale collection was saved. It is catalogued and preserved at the Simcoe County Archives, Midhurst, awaiting the opening of a heritage centre in Orillia.

ALVIN HAMILTON enjoyed a long career in Ottawa, serving as minister of agriculture from 1960 to 1963, after his stint as minister of northern affairs in the first Diefenbaker government. He returned to The Old Brewery Bay in 1983 to help mark its silver anniversary.

JAMES B. LAMB, the *Packet* publisher and fiery editorialist, retired from the paper in 1971 and moved to Big Harbour, Nova Scotia, where he turned out a string of best-sellers, among them *Corvette Navy, On The Triangle Run* and *Press Gang.* The latter was his autobiography. It depicted characters and events in Orillia in the fifties and sixties that were surprisingly Leacockian in style and content. One chapter is an affectionate portrait of C.H. Hale.

STEPHEN LEACOCK JR. declined the invitation to join the festivities at the opening of the Leacock home, although he did return occasionally to chat with Ralph Curry. Publicly he neither praised nor damned the restoration efforts. In 1970, the last time I saw him, he was an invalid, propped up in bed in a room at Orillia's Champlain Hotel, a table of assorted pills and potions at his side. A year earlier I had written a feature article for the *Packet* on the tenth anniversary of the home's opening. The day after the article appeared, in March 1969, Stevie phoned, furious. It was bad enough that I had referred to "squalor and neglect" at the home during his years in residence,[3] but that was not the reason he had phoned. He hated my description of him as "a little man." I had written no such thing. A check of the offending sentence showed me he had misread it. When I pointed out his error he dropped the belligerence and moved on to another topic, exactly as he had done so often during my visits to the lodge in 1955. On that final visit I found him a shrunken shadow of his former self. He died in Orillia on 26 September 1974, and was laid to rest in St. George's churchyard in Sutton, steps away from his father's grave. He was fifty-nine years old.

JEAN LESAGE, the Liberal minister of northern affairs who rejected an historical designation for the Leacock home in 1957, left federal politics in May 1958 to lead Quebec's provincial Liberals. Elected premier in 1960 he fathered the "Quiet Revolution," introducing far-reaching social and political reforms. Defeated in 1966, he served till 1970 as Opposition leader. He left office in 1970 and died 12 December 1980.

BARBARA (ULRICHSEN) NIMMO, Stephen Leacock's niece and secretary, travelled from her home in Michigan to The Old Brewery Bay almost every summer after 1958. She advised curator Ralph Curry on a thousand matters, from the meaning of obscure correspondence to the placement of furniture in the living room, all the while keeping a low profile. More than any other person, Barbara Nimmo was our link to the legend. It was a role she would continue to fill until she died of cancer on 18 June 1993 in Birmingham, Michigan.

LOUIS W. RUBY was an honoured guest on Opening Day at the Leacock home. He and his wife Marie unveiled the plaque erected by the Home Board to acknowledge his donation of the home's contents. The Rubys returned many times to The Old Brewery Bay. No houses were ever built in the Ruby subdivision and the property was sold to the city of Orillia in 1977 for $400,000. On 5 July 1983, at ceremonies marking the twenty-fifth anniversary of the opening of the Leacock home, Lou's son, civil rights champion Clayton Ruby, remarked that presenting the Leacock treasures to the town of Orillia was a highlight of his father's life – his way of saying "thank you" to a country that had opened its doors to a poor immigrant boy.

I continued to chair the Leacock Home Board till 1965, when I transferred to CFCO, Chatham, as news director. In 1973 I moved to Toronto as a featured newscaster/commentator on CKEY and remained for fourteen and a half years. On New Year's Day, 1988, Eileen and I semi-retired to a home on the north shore of Lake Simcoe, ten kilometres from Orillia. I felt my life had come full circle when city council appointed me to the Leacock Museum Board in 1991. The following year Eileen was elected a director of the Stephen Leacock Associates. In my Toronto years I acted as a program director and corporate canvasser for the Associates, lining up celebrities to host the dinners and companies to write cheques for the winner. In 1989 I proposed a new award – The Order of Mariposa – to honour creators of Canadian humour working in media other than books. Duncan MacPherson, the dean of Canadian political cartoonists, was inducted a few months before his death in 1993.

Leacock was the supreme ironist, and the history of his home is filled with ironies. Consider them – Orillia's thundering temperance advocate, C.H. Hale, as the champion of Canada's best-known tippler! Or Lou Ruby – he of the notorious scandal-sheet – saving the Leacock treasures of the Leacock home. Or Orillia ratepayers, voting not so much to acquire the Leacock home as to keep me on council. Or Leslie Frost – "Old Man Ontario" and Orillia's chief booster – turning a deaf ear to our pleas. Or Alvin Hamilton coming through with $15,000 to make amends for a bureaucratic blunder.

And this crowning irony, the one Leacock would have relished the most: the salvation of his home was accomplished, not through a great national campaign involving governments, foundations, philanthropists, McGill alumni or the rest of the academic community (all of whom were approached and all of whom backed away), but through the efforts of a clutch of stubborn Orillians, using some political moxie. Leacock would have loved that – his Mariposans showing the big sophisticated world how to get things done.

POSTSCRIPT

MEMORIES

BY JAY CODY, CURATOR, 1977–1993

"Lord Ronald flung himself from the room, flung himself upon his horse and rode madly off in all directions." Stephen Leacock, who gave us this hilarious image, might well have been describing the duties and responsibilities of a director/curator of the Stephen Leacock Museum. He or she must train and oversee staff, keep the books, maintain the archives, meet the media, work with the board in devising and implementing policies and try to maintain a civil relationship with civil authorities.

It's not always easy! My arrival at The Old Brewery Bay was the result of one uncivil incident, and there would be many more in the years to come. As Pete McGarvey notes in his concluding chapter, Ralph Curry's position became tenuous in 1976 because of a change in regulation concerning non-Canadians performing professional services here. For twenty years Ralph had laboured tirelessly every summer to restore the home and preserve and document the vast collection of Leacockiana it housed. He was beyond question the most eminent Leacock scholar of his day and far and away the most qualified director the home could hope for. Despite all that, the Leacock Memorial Home Board made it known that his days were numbered. That year I had retired from a lifetime in the resort business, and although I had always enjoyed reading Leacock, I could scarcely be considered an expert on him or qualified to direct the affairs of Orillia's unique literary museum. Nevertheless I applied for the position of curator, and soon found myself on a short list of seven applicants (Ralph Curry did not apply). But in the end, town council picked none of the final seven, opting instead to engage Toronto publicist Henry Janes, an old friend of the Leacock family who had once leased the Leacock property (see Chapter 3). The personable Janes was proposed by his close friend, Alderman Wilbur Cramp, a colourful former mayor who was the "Josh McCosh" of his day. I was appointed secretary/treasurer by the board to serve with Janes and Curry. Curry's term was to end at the close of 1976. He used his final summer to indoctrinate me into the techniques of running a small, underfunded literary museum. Henry Janes turned up rarely during the summer, though he never failed to collect his director's fees. In 1977 I was appointed acting director/curator. Janes was so outraged by this turn of events he cut all ties with the Leacock home. I was named full-time director/curator in 1978 when I had completed the Ontario Museums Association Studies Certificate course.

While I couldn't bring Ralph Curry's scholastic insight to the job, I could bring some ideas that would solidify the Leacock-Orillia connection, and generate some fun in the process. For instance, Stephen Leacock met his future wife, Beatrix Hamilton, in 1896 on the grass tennis court at Southwood, the palatial Orillia estate of her uncle, Major Henry Pellatt, the father of financier Sir Henry Pellatt, builder of that over-ripe architectural folly, Toronto's Casa Loma. Why not use that historic tidbit to establish an annual tennis tournament? We did, calling it the "Stephen and Trixie Mid-Summer Mixed Tennis Tournament." The Orillia Tennis club, where the match is played, was originally part of the Leacock estate. Similarly, Leacock had been an enthusiastic player with modest skills on the Orillia Cricket Team in the 1890s and so we launched the "Annual Stephen Butler Leacock Invitational Cricket Tournament." As Leacock had spent a lifetime of summers happily sailing the waters of Lakes Simcoe and Couchiching, we decided to memorialize this activity by establishing the "Annual Celebrated Mariposa Belle Yacht Race," co-sponsored by the Leacock Museum and the Brewery Bay Tennis and Sailing Club. The only objective of the competitors is to circumnavigate Sanson's Shoal – where the old steamer *Enterprise* once foundered, an incident that is said to have been the inspiration of the sinking of the *Mariposa Belle* in "The Marine Excursion of the Knights of Pythias" in *Sunshine Sketches* – and return safely in time for the barbecue. The winner is chosen through a complicated handicapping process that involves pulling a number out of an old straw hat. What happier way to spend a summer afternoon in Mariposa.

As Pete McGarvey has related, the town's 1957 purchase of the home and an adjoining acre of land for parking established our boundaries. Around us, everything was owned by the Ruby estate. Thankfully, a subdivision plan drawn up by Lou Ruby in 1958 never got off the ground. In 1977 the Ruby estate sold its entire acreage to the City of Orillia for $400,000. The city reserved the property for park development. Immediately the Leacock

Memorial Home Board petitioned the city to enlarge our meagre acreage as a means of guarding against future encroachment and to reflect the original setting. Council sat on the request. We asked again. And again. The Ontario Heritage Foundation appeared before the council with John Raynor as spokesman, but to no avail. The matter was delayed repeatedly, referred to committees, subjected to studies and to all intents and purposes simply ignored. Council's failure to consider the Leacock home as a definite cultural asset for the city was to lead to serious problems in the future.

On our own initiative, without requesting official approval and despite the uncertainty about the ultimate disposition of the property, we began to clear the heavy growth surrounding the home and extend the lawns to the east. This opened up for the first time the beautiful vista of Barnfield Bay and beyond. Because of budget constraints, it took more than three years to complete. We were grateful for the donation of labour by inmates from Camp Hillsdale Correctional Centre, which helped defray the cost. Behind the home to the south, the property was cleared as far as the double row of mature cedars that had been planted by Leacock to separate the home and gardens used by the Leacock family and their guests from what was a working farm. Later, with the aid of a provincial grant, we reconstructed Leacock's garden arbour and his personal vegetable garden.

Orillia City Council may have been indifferent to Leacock, but the same did not hold true for the general public. By the early 1980s we had doubled annual attendance from the museum's first years. According to my museum training, a visitor can be defined as "a pedestrian whose feet hurt, who is tired and preoccupied and who is on his way somewhere else." To beat boredom and fatigue a museum's exhibits must be arresting, instructive and entertaining. As they told us in class, "it has to make them feel good." Our Mariposa Room, housed in the easternmost upstairs bedroom, did the trick. Every visitor treasures the details of small-town life, the recollection in *Sunshine Sketches of a Little Town*. In this bedroom we assembled photographs and mementos of Leacock's Orillia at the turn of the century. Here are the real people Leacock transformed into characters known and loved by millions the world over. People linger in the Mariposa Room. We wanted to do more, but our money ran out.

The City of Orillia didn't neglect us entirely in the 1970s. It gave us a bus, a retired transit coach, to use as a gift shop and a haven for our young interpretative guides. For years this derelict sank deeper and deeper into the mud of the parking lot and became an acute embarrassment, though gift shop sales were soaring. Something had to be done. In 1981 we drew up plans for a resource centre, complete with washrooms, audio-visual facilities, a tearoom and a proper gift-shop. We asked the city to help but got the expected answer. The city met its obligation to support our operating budget, but capital funding was always a problem. Replacing a collapsing porch could turn into a major money battle at City Hall. The Ontario Ministry of Culture and Communications was more sympathetic. A grant allowed us to complete the first phase, a brand-new gift shop. The old city bus was hauled from the mud and sent to the City Bus Cemetery. Meantime, the city fathers were considering offers on the former Ruby acreage, and that had us worried. John Carter, museum development officer of the Ministry of Culture and Communications, expressed his concern in a letter to council that read in part, "we trust that the city of Orillia will bear in mind the historic integrity of the Leacock home and the lands surrounding it, as future plans for the Ruby property are considered." The advise was sound, but completely ignored.

Sixteen developers responded to the city's invitation to bid on the land. Ultimately the nod went to Versa Care's pledge to come up with $350,000, in lieu of parkland, to be used by the Leacock Museum, at the discretion of city council. The Cambridge, Ontario, company planned to build a continuing-care facility for seniors. Lord knows we needed this kind of cash infusion, but more urgently we needed a definition of our boundaries, the question council had been avoiding for ten years. How close would Versa Care's subdivision come to the home? That was the key question. Although we were finally accorded representation on the City Development Committee, set up to deal with the technical side of Versa Care's proposals, it wasn't till the agreement was formally signed and a press conference called that we learned what city fathers had decided on our behalf. The greater part of the south lawn, in addition to the newly constructed arbour, would be lost. In addition, a large settling pond was to be positioned on the east arm of the bay, a place of pristine beauty known as Leacock Point. The desecration of the site shocked and angered many Orillians, who quickly formed "The Committee to Protect the Leacock Home." The battle was joined.

Discussions and negotiations eliminated the settling-pond proposal. The alternative – no great improvement – was a channel to carry run-off directly into the wetlands of the bay. After several meetings Versa Care also pulled back a bit on the boundary, although not enough to mollify the Committee to Protect. Tempers heated up; tensions rose. Mayor John Palmer, at seven foot, three inches the tallest free-standing chief magistrate in Canada, ran out of patience with the committee and the Leacock Home Board. It was rumoured he favoured a convenient fire at The Old Brewery Bay as the right solution. The committee applied for legal aid to organize an appeal to the Ontario Municipal Board. The city's solicitor tried – but failed – to block the application. Two aldermen, in a lather of indignation, declared publicly that no member of the Committee to Protect, or members of their families, would ever be employed by the city. It was a hollow threat. It's interesting to note that the chairman of the Committee to Protect, Gwen Richardson, became a valued member of the Leacock Museum Board in 1991. The issues and questions the committee raised were finally resolved at a five-day meeting of the Ontario Municipal Board held at the Orillia council chambers in May of 1989. The board ruled in favour of the city and Versa Care in general, but stipulated a space of at least 66 metres (216.7 feet) must be left between the Leacock Museum and the nearest subdivision homes. A curious interpretation of this ruling by the city and the developer, accepted by the Ontario Municipal Board, reduced this distance to only 48.5 metres (158 feet). My protest at what I regarded as manipulation of the intent of the OMB ruling so infuriated Rick Willis, the president of Versa Care, that he demanded the Museum Board suppress my "malicious rantings" and my "loose tongue."

Through the 1980s, with the earnest support of Simcoe North member of Parliament Doug Lewis, we had petitioned the National Historic Sites and Monuments Board to designate The Old Brewery Bay a National Historic Site. For almost thirty years we assumed we already carried that title, but that was a misunderstanding. As Pete McGarvey relates, the home's restoration was made possible by a timely grant from Ottawa in 1958. Four days before the home opened, directional signs arrived, bearing the words "Historic Site" under the Canadian coat of arms. Didn't that mean the home was a National Historic Site? The administrators of the day thought so and promotional literature advertised the place as such for many years. But they were mistaken and premature by thirty years. In April 1989, we tried to put things right. With Doug Lewis's assistance, an appointment was made to discuss the designation in Ottawa, and as a matter of courtesy the mayor of Orillia was informed of our intentions. To our astonishment a firestorm erupted at City Hall. It was now the turn of Mayor Palmer and the city council to "ride madly off in all directions." An emergency council meeting was called to discuss appropriate disciplinary measures to be taken against the director of the Stephen Leacock Museum! The director's sin? His contact with Ottawa was clearly obstructionist. He was trying to block council's decision to give the Versa Care development a green light. Cooler heads eventually prevailed. While this first application to the National Historic Sites and Monuments Board failed, we urged the secretary general of the National Historic Sites Board, Christina Cameron, to reconsider and invited her to spend the weekend of the 1991 Leacock Medal Dinner in Orillia as our guest. A brilliantly composed report by researcher Hillary Russell of Parks Canada won them over. On 26 June 1994 Chairman Thomas Symons of the National Historic

Sites and Monuments Board presided at ceremonies to declare The Old Brewery Bay a National Historic Site.

It was finally official. The home is unique – the only place in Canada where two National Historic Plaques are placed side by side, one honouring the greatest of our humorists, the other acknowledging the significance of his home in the Canadian cultural landscape. It was a proud and joyous day, coinciding with another Leacock home tradition, the Annual Garden Party.

Not all my encounters with city fathers have been confrontational, and I have to say, despite differences over the years, I remain on cordial terms with most of our elected officials. If I was intransigent from time to time, it was nothing personal. I was simply trying to fill a part of my mandate spelled out in the job description – the protection of the integrity of Orillia's Leacock legacy.

I was in the soup again soon after the Versa Care development began. In preparing the site, the developer had deposited two thousand truck loads of powdery fill, covering Leacock's fields and orchards to an average depth of eight feet. The dust stirred up by the trucks and bulldozers posed a serious threat to the museum's archives and public access was hazardous. Things got so bad we had to close our doors and move our precious papers (including the most valued manuscript in Canada – *Sunshine Sketches of a Little Town*) to the Simcoe County Archives in Midhurst. The problem, which could have been easily mitigated by the developer, caught the attention of the national media.

By this date, plans for the long-delayed resource centre were well advanced. How much we had to spend was uncertain, as discussions went back and forth with Versa Care on the terms of their grant. At a meeting on 9 April 1990, Simon Broughton, Versa Care's project manager, assured us the cost of extending city services to the home would *not* exceed $50,000 and would be computed from the Leacock property lot line. We were stunned when the development company demanded $164,000 for the services it was extending to the home, putting our plans for the resource centre in serious jeopardy. City negotiators eventually settled for $80,000. Part of the Versa Care grant, combined with a Jobs Ontario grant of $148,000 (promoted by MPP Al MacLean and confirmed on 30 July 1993), made possible a handsome structure, complete with an environmentally controlled Archive Room, a feature urged by the Ontario Ministry of Culture and Communications after our summer of ruinous dust.

The ground-breaking ceremony for Swanmore Hall took place on 19 November 1992. It was an important milestone in the history of The Old Brewery Bay. What took shape over the next seven months was a spacious and beautiful facility, architecturally in harmony with the home itself.

Swanmore Hall, named in honour of the village in Hampshire, England, where Stephen Leacock was born, was designed by Rod Young of Orillia. We engaged a project manager not only to control costs but to ensure that local contractors would be part of the process. Wesley Trinier, vice chairman of the Leacock Museum Board, headed the building committee and deserves credit and praise for the meticulous attention he gave every detail. Within weeks of its opening it had become Orillia's favourite social rendezvous. The patio facing the bay is considered the most inspiring view of Lake Couchiching to be found.

The footpath that borders the bay, in a grassy area north of the patio, was the subject of another "misunderstanding" between city officials and the Museum Board. That path is part of the Lightfoot Trail, a walking and cycling pathway which follows a course from Orillia's northern border along the waterfront to Tudhope Park, east of The Old Brewery Bay. Since the earliest meetings of the City Trail Committee in 1981, we had rejected their plan to cross the environmentally sensitive wetlands west of Swanmore Hall and the restored lawns of the Leacock home. We repeatedly pointed out to city officials the need to satisfy whatever standards and restrictions provincial and federal governments imposed on heritage properties in which they had a declared interest. As time passed, the discussions escalated into a battle of wills – and again tempers were frayed. I objected strongly and publicly when the path was bulldozed along the newly sodded shoreline beside Swanmore Hall, though I was no longer the home's curator. I'm convinced that only the timely intervention of John Lewis, director of the Trent Severn Waterway, Parks Canada, stopped the path from crossing the lawns directly in front of the Leacock home.

The museum's long-time administrative assistant, Doris Medlock, retired in 1990 and the search for a replacement attracted forty-one applicants. Daphne Mainprize was selected. She brought enthusiasm, commitment and interpersonal and marketing skills to the management team. A marketing cooperative with the Opera House and the *Island Princess* supported by Daphne and me resulted in an increase of 83 percent in our visitor count in 1991. I was delighted that the board saw fit to appoint Daphne as my successor in 1993.

The transition of Stephen Leacock's 1928 home from a few rooms opened for a two-month summer season in 1958 to the internationally recognized literary museum of today, open the year round, is a matter of great satisfaction to all of us who have played a part in this venture. Our attendance has increased 500 percent in the course of twenty years! A close and friendly relationship with residents of the nearby seniors development has led to many joint activities (now that the dust, literally, has settled). Our registry shows guests from every corner of the globe. VIPs arrive regularly. In my time we have welcomed Governor General Edward Schreyer and his family, Prime Minister Jean Chrétien, authors Pierre Berton, W.O, Mitchell, Peter Gzowski, Timothy Findley and scores more. The Old Brewery Bay is an authentic haven for Canada's writers and Leacock would be pleased. He also would be pleased to know that his kinfolk have made the pilgrimage: the late Barbara Nimmo, his niece and one-time secretary; writer Elizabeth Kimball, another niece very much in the Leacock mould; and Richard Burrowes, a nephew with recollections of happy days at a beautiful spot.

For eighteen years I have lived with the kindly, mischievous ghost of Stephen Leacock, surrounded by the things that formed the substance of his life. His rambling nineteen-room summer house, his books, his letters, his pictures – even his very voice on tape that drifted through the familiar rooms as he narrated a whimsical tale. The enchantment lives on at The Old Brewery Bay.

APPENDIX

WINNERS OF THE
STEPHEN LEACOCK MEDAL AWARD FOR HUMOUR

Year	Author	Title	Publisher
1947	Harry L. Symons	*Ojibway Melody*	Ambassador
1948	Paul Hiebert	*Sarah Binks*	Oxford University Press
1949	Angeline Hango	*Truthfully Yours*	Oxford University Press
1950	Earle Birney	*Turvey*	McClelland and Stewart
1951	Eric Nichol	*The Roving I*	Ryerson Press
1952	Jan Hilliard	*The Salt-Box*	McLeod (Norton)
1953	Lawrence Earl	*The Battle of Baltinglass*	Clarke Irwin
1954	Joan Walker	*Pardon My Parka*	McClelland and Stewart
1955	Robertson Davies	*Leaven of Malice*	Clarke Irwin
1956	Eric Nicol	*Shall We Join the Ladies?*	Ryerson Press
1957	Robert Thomas Allen	*The Grass Is Never Greener*	McClelland and Stewart
1958	Eric Nicol	*Girdle Me a Globe*	Ryerson Press
1959	No award made		
1960	Pierre Berton	*Just Add Water and Stir*	McClelland and Stewart
1961	Norman Ward	*Mice in the Beer*	Longmans
1962	W.O. Mitchell	*Jake and the Kid*	Macmillan of Canada
1963	Donald Jack	*Three Cheers for Me*	Collier-Macmillan
1964	Harry J. Boyle	*Homebrew and Patches*	Clarke Irwin
1965	Gregory Clark	*War Stories*	Ryerson Press
1966	George Bain	*Nursery Rhymes to Be Read Aloud by Young Parents with Old Children*	Clarke Irwin
1967	Richard J. Needham	*Needham's Inferno*	Macmillan of Canada
1968	Max Ferguson	*And Now … Here's Max*	McGraw-Hill
1969	Stuart Trueman	*You're Only As Old As You Act*	McClelland and Stewart
1970	Farley Mowat	*The Boat Who Wouldn't Float*	McClelland and Stewart

1971	Robert Thomas Allen	*Wives, Children and Other Wildlife*	Paper Jacks
1972	Max Braithwaite	*The Night They Stole the Mounties' Car*	McClelland and Stewart
1973	Donald Bell	*Saturday Night at the Bagel Factory*	McClelland and Stewart
1974	Donald Jack	*That's Me in the Middle*	Doubleday
1975	Morley Torgov	*A Good Place to Come From*	Lester and Orpen
1976	Harry J. Boyle	*The Luck of the Irish*	Macmillan
1977	Ray Guy	*That Far Greater Bay*	Breakwater Books
1978	Ernest Buckler	*Whirligig*	McClelland and Stewart
1979	Sondra Gotlieb	*True Confessions*	Musson
1980	Donald Jack	*Me Bandy, You Cissie*	Doubleday
1981	Gary Lautens	*Take My Family ... Please*	John Wiley and Sons/Madison Press Books
1982	Mervyn J. Huston	*Gophers Don't Pay Taxes*	Tree Frog Press
1983	Morley Torgov	*The Outside Chance of Maximilian Glick*	Lester & Orpen Dennys
1984	Gary Lautens	*No Sex Please ... We're Married*	McClelland and Stewart
1985	Ted Allan	*Love Is a Long Shot*	McClelland and Stewart
1986	Joey Slinger	*No Axe Too Small to Grind*	McClelland and Stewart
1987	W.P. Kinsella	*The Fencepost Chronicles*	Totem Press/Collins Publishers
1988	Paul Quarrington	*King Leary*	Doubleday
1989	Joseph Kertes	*Winter Tulips*	Doubleday
1990	W.O. Mitchell	*According to Jake and the Kid*	McClelland and Stewart
1991	Howard White	*Writing in the Rain*	Harbour Publishing
1992	Roch Carrier	*Prayers for a Very Wise Child*	Penguin Books Canada
1993	John Levesque	*Waiting for Aquarius*	Mosaic Press Publishers
1994	Bill Richardson	*Bachelor Brothers Bed & Breakfast*	Douglas & McIntyre

NOTES

Introduction

1. Stephen Leacock, "Sunshine Skits," 1943. The skits were syndicated in a number of daily newspapers. This skit appeared in the 5 May 1943 edition of the Toronto *Telegram*.

Chapter One: The Old Brewery Bay

1. Margaret (Daisy) Burrowes's account of early years at Old Brewery Bay is the only eye-witness record available. According to her daughter, Elizabeth Kimball, her mother revised the article a number of times in her last years. A typescript in Kimball's possession, dated 1957, is titled "Stephen Leacock's House at Old Brewery Bay." Excerpts quoted in this chapter are found in Grace Crooks, "A Taste for Humour," *Canadian Library Journal* 26:3 (May-June 1969), 222–24, and in Elizabeth Kimball, *My Uncle, Stephen Leacock* (Halifax: Goodread Biographies, 1983), originally published under the title *The Man in the Panama Hat* (Toronto: McClelland & Stewart, 1970).
2. Abstract, Bargain and Sale, Registered mortgage, 16 April 1908, Simcoe County Land Registry Office, Barrie.
3. Ralph Curry, *Stephen Leacock, Humorist and Humanist* (Garden City, New York: Doubleday and Co., 1959), 74
4. Barbara Nimmo, Preface to *Last Leaves* (Toronto: McClelland and Stewart, 1945), xx.
5. Kimball, *My Uncle, Stephen Leacock,* 58, 59, 60, 61.
6. Orillia *Packet,* 22 May 1908. Leacock's speech to his fellow Orillians was his first delivered anywhere after the 1907 Commonwealth tour, a matter of great pride to the *Packet*'s editor.
7. C.H. Hale, Speech ("Origins of characters in Sunshine Sketches of a Little Town"), 14 September 1951, delivered at Leacock Medal Dinner. The Hale brothers, Harold and Russell of the *Packet,* appear in *Sunshine Sketches* as "Hussell," a reporter for the *Newspacket.*
8. Hale, Memorandum "Orillia, The Sunshine Town," 1948, Stephen Leacock Associate Archives, Orillia Public Library.
9. Ibid.

10.   Letter, Kenneth Noxon to Ralph Curry, 25 June 1959, in possession of Court Noxon.

11.   Allan Anderson, *Remembering Leacock* (Ottawa: Deneau Publishers, 1983), 99.

12.   Ibid., 114.

13.   Kimball, *My Uncle, Stephen Leacock*, 56.

14.   Correspondence File, Stephen Leacock Museum Archives, 15 July 1930.

15.   Stephen Leacock, "Come Out into the Garden," *The Leacock Roundabout* (New York: Dodd Mead and Co., 1972), 169.

16.   After the death of his wife, Trix, in 1925, Leacock invited his niece Barbara Ulrichsen, then living in Massachusetts, to join his household in Montreal and complete her university education at McGill. He would pay for her courses. In exchange she would serve as his secretary, confidante and friend, an experience she once described as "a bit like living beside a volcano." Following her death in 1993 David Staines observed in a tribute published in the *Newspacket*, the Leacock Associates newsletter, "The respect and love between uncle and niece only deepened as Barbara Ulrichsen became indispensable to her uncle's life."

17.   Nimmo, Preface to *Last Leaves*, xxi.

18.   This story was told by Leacock's Montreal friend Henry Mainer at a Leacock Medal dinner in the early 1950s attended by the author. Mainer told many such tales over the years, some obviously embellished, but all entertaining.

19.   Kimball, *My Uncle, Stephen Leacock*, 88.

20.   From taped conversation with Yousuf Karsh, 17 February 1992.

Chapter Two: C.H. Hale, The Catalyst

1.   C.H. Hale "Genesis of the Water, Light and Power Commission," *Reminiscences* (Orillia: Stubley Printing 1963, privately published), 49.

2.   "Leacock's Connection with Orillia," Orillia *Packet and Times*, 12 March 1957. (Note: The article is a transcript of the CBC broadcast. After 1925 the Orillia *Packet* became the Orillia *Packet and Times* – hence the two different citations for the same newspaper.)

3.   Ibid.

4.   "Tribute to Stephen Leacock," Orillia *Packet and Times*, 6 April 1944.

5.   Robertson Davies, "Diary of an Optimist" by Samuel Marchbanks, *Kingston Whig-Standard*, 8 April 1944.

6.   Information on the first days of the Stephen Leacock Memorial Committee is drawn from the archives of the Stephen Leacock Associates at the Orillia Public Library.

Chapter Three: Saving the Leacock Home, 1949

1.   Orillia *News-Letter*, 13 February 1949.

2.   Ibid.

3. News release: Public Relation Services, Toronto, June 1949.
4. Ibid.
5. *Montreal Standard Weekend Magazine*, 8 October 1949.
6. Ibid.
7. Letter, Stephen Leacock Jr. to Editor, Montreal *Standard*, October 1949 (date unknown), copied by Orillia *Newsletter*, 20 October 1949.
8. Letter, Stephen Leacock Jr. to Editor, Orillia *Packet and Times*, 15 October 1949.

Chapter Four: The Leacock Cause, 1949–1955

1. Editorial, Orillia *Packet and Times*, 15 September 1951.
2. Deacon (1890–1977) served as the link between the Leacock Memorial Committee and the literary community. He framed the rules for the award of the Leacock Medal for Humour, enlisted the support of the Canadian Authors Association, promoted the award vigorously and recruited judges for the competition.
3. Stephen Leacock, "The Hostelry of Mr. Smith," *Sunshine Sketches of a Little Town*.
4. "No Sunshine Sketches For Queen," Toronto *Telegram*, 7 July 1953.
5. Ibid.
6. Griffith Bingham's father, Horace, was Orillia's leading undertaker in the first years of the twentieth century and the inspiration, in name at least, for Golgotha Gingham in *Sunshine Sketches*.
7. "No Laughing Matter; Mayor Chides Council," Orillia *Packet and Times*, 30 October 1954.
8. James B. Lamb, *Press Gang* (Toronto: Macmillan of Canada, 1979), 87.
9. Editorial, Orillia *Packet and Times*, 14 November 1954.
10. "All Our Yesterdays," Montreal *Gazette*, 10 September 1955.
11. Ibid.
12. Ibid.
13. Orillia *News-Letter*, 6 December 1955.
14. Ibid.
15. Curry's enthusiasm for The Old Brewery Bay and its treasures is expressed in a letter to the author 10 October 1955.

Chapter Five: Lou Ruby Strikes a Deal, 1956

1. "Looking Down on Brewery Bay," column by Wessely Hicks, Toronto *Telegram*, 31 January 1956.
2. Letter, W.B. Greenwood to H.E.M. Payne, Clerk Treasurer, Town of Orillia, 5 September 1956.
3. "Reeve Drops out of Race," Orillia *Packet and Times*, 20 November 1956.
4. Letter, C.H. Hale to author, 11 December 1956.

Chapter Six: Waiting on Ottawa, 1957

1. Orillia *Packet and Times*, 29 January 1957.
2. Letter from the author to A.J.H. Richardson, 17 May 1957, contains references to January discussion of options and March meeting with Jean Lesage.
3. Orillia Parks Board presentation to the National Historic Sites and Monuments Board, Ottawa, June 1957.
4. Minutes, National Historic Sites and Monuments Board, June 1957.
5. Ibid.
6. Ibid.
7. Ibid.
8. Letter, Professor Fred Landon to author, 22 November 1957.
9. Editorial, Orillia *Packet and Times*, 12 January 1958.
10. "Off to Ottawa," Orillia *Packet and Times*, 23 January 1958.
11. "Reception Favourable to Leacock Memorial," Orillia *Packet and Times*, 24 January 1958.

Chapter Seven: A Dream Comes True, 1958

1. Details of the 1957 restoration are contained in a letter from the author to Ralph Curry, 17 May 1957. Curry was still in Kentucky.
2. Orillia *Packet and Times*, 7 July 1958.
3. Wessely Hicks, "Champlain Trod Here," Toronto *Telegram*, 7 July 1958.

Chapter Eight: The Dream Expands, 1959–1960

1. Town of Orillia By-law 3627, 29 May 1958.
2. In a presentation to Orillia Town Council, 10 November 1960, the Leacock Memorial Home Board estimated that it would take ten years and $50,000 to complete restoration of the Leacock property. Plans included buying more land around the home from Ruby, extensive landscaping, and promotion of Leacock-related activities. We even proposed the revival of Leacock's "East Simcoe Anti-Mosquito League" as a money-raising venture.

Chapter Nine: Aftermath

1. Laurie McKechnie, "Doctor Leacock's Tonic Helps Queen," Toronto *Telegram*, 25 July 1959.
2. Book review, William Arthur Deacon, Toronto *Globe and Mail*, 31 October 1959.
3. J.A. McGarvey, "Story of Stephen Leacock Memorial Home," Orillia *Packet and Times*, March 1969.